DOCUMENTS
ON THE MEXICAN REVOLUTION

Volume VI

OTHER VOLUMES IN THIS SERIES

¡ABAJO EL GRINGO!

Anti-American Sentiment During the Mexican Revolution

Edited & Introduced
by
Gene Z. Hanrahan

DOCUMENTARY PUBLICATIONS
Salisbury, North Carolina, U.S.A.
1982

INTRODUCTION

This collection of fifty-eight letters, documents, reports and telegrams depicts the real and imagined plight of Americans caught up in the first years of the Mexican Revolution. These are important accounts. Not only do they contain significant historical material, but they provide as well additional fragments to a complex mosaic vividly depicting the confusion, rage and fear which characterized the thousands of Americans caught up in this bloody and chaotic struggle.

The authors of these documents were of many vocations and political persuasions: some were diplomats; others were businessmen, settlers, ranchers or mine managers. Some supported the revolutionaries; most, however, were on the side of the established government and economic power base. But all had one common purpose in these writings: to inform friends, business associates, congressmen or government officials of the true nature of the revolution as they saw it. Throughout these writings was the idea that somehow the Americans and the U.S. Government could play a role in determining the course of the Mexican Revolution -- either through specific action, or intentional inaction. The writers voiced their ideas, concerns and recommendations. And each sought, in his own way, to suggest ways and means by which the Americans living and working in Mexico might not only survive the killing, but hold on to their influence, lands and businesses.

Unfortunately, one critical question remains unanswered in these materials. Was the anti-Americanism in the Mexican Revolution more brutal and more extreme than the anti-foreign feelings found in any revolution? When one considers the unique circumstances, a firm conclusion on one side or the other is difficult. Certainly the United States was, at that time, the most influential foreign power in Mexico. The United States Government maintained close ties with Porfirio Diaz and his administration. And American businessmen and settlers controlled a large portion of the Mexican economy, particularly in the key northern states. No one can deny the American role in the development of and control over Mexican railroads, communications, banking, oi , agricultural enterprises and mining. By 1910, economic Mexico – and much of its political base – was closely related to or dominated by American interests.

Under these conditions it is difficult to see how the revolutionaries could divorce the Diaz administration from American business and governmental interests. Perhaps one could even argue that the revolutionaries showed remarkable restraint under such conditions. Surely to many, Diaz and Americanism were one and the same. To end political and economic exploitation, one had to attack as well the real support of Diaz – the Yankee.

Contrarily, it can be demonstrated that a portion of the revolutionaries were not motivated in their behavior by purely humane motives. While they believed that America and Americans constituted a sizeable part of the problem in Mexico, they also realized that much of their financial and moral support must come from the north. The revolutionaries could not afford to so alienate public opinion in the United States that all possibility of aid might be cut off. Even more critical was the ever-present threat of military intervention. Few doubted that such an intervention, if energetically pursued, would all but end the revolution and thereby Mexico's hopes for social, economic and political change.

The fifty-eight documents in this volume make no pretense of providing definitive answers to these questions. The serious scholar must search more deeply for his answer. A wealth of original source materials are to be found in the vast number of government hearings and reports treating American claims for losses to life and property as a result of the Revolution. Both American and Mexican government repositories bulge with these rich sources. One must also consult the extensive contemporary body of literature produced by the revolutionaries and their leaders. Several hundred memoirs and autobiographies deal in some measure with this issue. Then, of course, there are the Mexican scholarly histories produced over the past forty years, particularly those relating to Mexico's relations with the United States. One could go on and on. But even then a final resolution to this question is at best only probable. The emotions of those days ran deep, the facts were colored by the bias of the writers, and much of the real truth may remain buried in the past.

As with the documents presented in earlier volumes in this series, all materials included in this work have been reproduced from original papers preserved in the U.S. National Archives in Washington, D.C. All materials have been presented, as far as possible, in their original form, without substantive alterations or additions.

Gene Z. Hanrahan

CONTENTS

OCCIDENTAL CONSTRUCTION COMPANY
Office No. 704
64 Wall Street

Lewis Warfield
    President

                                    New York
                                    April 20, 1911

To the Honorable
        William H. Taft,
            President of the United States
                Washington.

Mr. President:

Will you kindly permit me to say a word or two in respect to the Mexican situation. My bona fides are: - My Company owns more real estate in the County of Tamazula, State of Durango, Mexico, than any other foreigner, and my personal relations with the Mexican Government are most cordial. The latter statement will be evident to you, I think, if you will read the enclosed letters of recent date received by me from Minister Limantour and Minister Vera Estanol, which I beg you will kindly return. I am making this use of Mr. Limantour's letter without first having obtained his permission, because I am sure that my motive justifies it. Minister Vera Estanol has been my Counsel at Mexico City for several years.

My knowledge of affairs in Mexico is not based upon "information and belief", but upon direct knowledge acquired by years of personal contact with all classes of Mexican people, both in business intercourse and in social intercourse. I first wish to offer you my sincere congratulations upon the evident sincerity and earnestness with which you are endeavoring to prevent any interference in the internal contest, notwithstanding the under-currents that have been set in motion to sway you into interference.

The few words that I ask your consideration to are these:

The bulk of the fifteen million Mexicans are untutored and are readily swayed in times of excitement by false prophets and demagogues, because they cannot read and they live a minutely circumscribed life. There has been a latent distrust as to the friendly intentions of the United States toward Mexico for some years past, more particularly since we acquired Panama. This distrust has now become acute by many causes, chief among which is the active participation by so many so-called American citizens in the ranks of the insurrectionists, and by the almost flagrant sympathy and aid extended to the insurrectionists by Americans and Mexicans residing in the south-western part of our country. These same charges, if made by the Mexican Government, ought to be thoroughly and impartially investigated.

The sincerity and integrity of men like General Diaz and Mr. Limantour cannot for a moment be doubted by any foreigner who has ever transacted any business matters with either of those gentlemen, as you know; and the fact that our Government and the bulk of our people are of that same belief is too clearly manifested to admit of any reasonable doubt on the part of people of intelligence or good motives anywhere. Nevertheless, it is, unfortunately, of advantage at the present moment, to a part of the upper classes in Mexico, that this distrust of our intentions should be fostered, and when demagogues appeal to the understanding of the untutored they make it appear to those people as if the American Government is really behind these so-called American citizens and American sympathizers, and that the motive of our Government is to take Mexico. All the World knows that we, as a Nation, have no monopoly upon the virtues of impartial justice and equal opportunity.

Very shortly, therefore, the slogan may be sounded "Out With The Gringoes", and the great bulk of the Mexican people either will not or cannot distinguish between Americans who have been neutral and those who have not been neutral. Such a situation will be only comparable to a religious war in the Oriental countries; and however much the Government of Mexico would deplore the situation, it is obvious to any man of intelligence that it would be impotent, of itself, to put it down. No matter what the final outcome would be, Americans would forever be regarded as traditional enemies of Mexico, and the citizens of all other nations would benefit at our expense in every possible manner. We should not pull the chestnuts out of the fire for the benefit of other foreigners, at the loss of our own standing. Mexico has benefitted greatly by our Monroe Doctrine, as is evidenced in part by the fact that she has no expensive Navy; but there seems to be a fear on the part of some of the population that the Monroe Doctrine makes us a special policeman for all foreigners domiciled on the American continent, and it is resented accordingly.

Don Quixote is not altogether a fictitious individual in Mexico. A great many Mexicans of the class forming the Rurales and the mountaineers sincerely believe that Mexico could whip the United States on our own territory, if it were not for Texas. They get that conviction by ignorance and also various legends; but, I am sorry to say, they come in contact with some pretty poor specimens of humanity who prowl about Mexico with the United States forever on their tongue but not in evidence in their appearance or conduct. It is not so surprising that this class of Mexicans have such notions, when we reflect that the geographies taught in the parochial schools belonging to some of the religious orders in Spain at the time of the Spanish-American War, pictured the United States as it was at the time of our Revolution in 1776; that is to say, with a fringe of population along the Atlantic Coast and a thickly populated Spanish portion beyond the Mississippi River to the Pacific Ocean. So that, when that fictitious interview attributed to General Weyler was circulated in Spain, wherein he was made to say that he could take the United States with fifty thousand soldiers if the Government would land them on the Coast of Florida, it did not seem incredible to the majority of the people. Fortunately, the "if" was not available.

My personal belief is, that if you would issue a short, clearcut proclamation, couched in the plainest and most unequivocal language possible, announcing the fact that our Government is not behind, or in sympathy with, any American citizens who are participating, either directly or indirectly, in Mexico's internal quarrel, and giving fair notice to Americans residing at home or abroad that our armed forces, consuls and administrative officers shall not be used to save them from the consequences of deliberate acts of interference or encouragement in any disorder, such a proclamation would reach the understanding and meet the approval of all patriotic citizens, both Americans and Mexicans. No reasonable expense should be spared to have this proclamation printed in every newspaper in Mexico and to have it circulated in every possible manner throughout that country.

I hope, Mr. President, you will regard what I have to say as evidencing my sincere desire to aid and uphold in some practical way, so far as my small efforts can go, the temperate course and good will that you have publicly manifested in your acts and statements.

Respectfully yours,

(signed) Lewis Warfield

[Enclosure not included.]

AMERICAN CONSULAR SERVICE
Veracruz, Mex.

January 25, 1912.

Honorable Henry Lane Wilson,
    American Ambassador,
        MEXICO.

Sir:

I have the honor to submit the following report on the political situation in this district, in compliance with instructions contained in a circular letter to consular officers from the Embassy, dated December 16, 1911, received December 21, 1911.

The State of Veracruz is as yet a field of contention between the numerous political agitators and office seekers for the spoils to be acquired by the change effected in the Federal government due to the recent revolution. Since Sr. Teodoro A. Dehesa relinguished the governorship, five or six others have provisionally held that post, the present incumbent being Sr. Manuel M. Alegre, and against whom there are already rumors of dissatisfaction current, that are becoming more clamorous from day to day.

As in the State so in municipal affairs, the changes in officials are so rapid and frequent that it is almost impossible to follow them. This is the case all over the interior towns and villages, especially so in Orizaba, Jalapa, Cordoba and that district back of Tuxpan, an almost isolated region, whenever a government position is involved. There is no denying the fact that the people at large seem to have the idea that they are to run this government now to the exclusion of all who may by education, capacity and social standing be above their level. This was particularly exemplified by the appointment of a clerk in a hardware store of Veracruz to the position of provisional governor of the State; a person who, in spite of the opposition made by the better classes did succeed in holding his position for a much longer time than did any of the others. The party in question has not even entree to respectable society.

In the industrial centers and where factory hands are found in great number, strikes after strikes have taken place. No sooner had an agreement been arranged between the owners and the operatives, when agitators stirred up the people anew and with the usual consequence. There is no doubt but that in some instances the people had just cause for dissatisfaction on the score of wages and working hours. This in combination with the system of supplying the needs of the workingmen from company storehouses also. But, in many instances these differences had been settled between owners and workers, and if the unprincipled political demagogues and professional mob leaders were not continually exciting the people with the sole object of prolonging the almost chaotic conditions and to their pecuniary advantage, quiet could have been restored long ago, for many concessions had been made to the workers. We are informed that all strikers have returned to work.

Very little information from the agricultural parts of this district reaches this office. That there is a general dissatisfaction and much discontent abroad is evident, but the precise reasons for this feeling cannot be stated to a certainty. Every few days political uprisings are reported from all parts of the interior. Some of these are confirmed, but rarely ever are any such reports contradicted after publication, and hence it seems to be the aim of certain publications to continue fomenting the excitement of the masses whenever comparative tranquility reigns, for the papers referred to never lose an opportunity when news is scarce to issue their papers with tremendous headlines calculated to revive the rancor and hate against foreigners, and especially Americans. Their articles are cunningly contrived and beyond the comprehension of the average working man, who but sees the heavy, black headlines, calculated to deceive him, nothing more. By way of variation and whenever other news items run short, the bugbear of American intervention is brought to the front. During the recent political agitation in Cuba, intervention was accomplished fast according to the local press. This furnished splendid material for them to publish articles to vent their spleen upon our government in malicious innuendos, usually clothed in sarcastic, sneering and taunting language. This work has been carried to the extent that even women declared themselves ready to take up arms against the hated "Gringo". Naturally, threats of violence have not been lacking, but with one or two exceptions nothing serious has happened. On the surface at least everything is quiet in the city at present.

The approaching elections for governor, set for Jan. 28, next, is the occasion for much personal abuse between the two opposing factions and levelled at the candidates. There are two prominently before the public, by means of the press, large posters, handbills, circulars and so called meetings, one of whom is Lic. Francisco Lagos Chazaro, and the other Gabriel Gavira. As his title indicates, the former seems to be a person of at least some qualifications for the office of governor, meanwhile the latter is reported to be a carpenter by trade and a self styled general of the usual stripe. It would be futile to make the attempt to foretell the result of this election. Gavira evidently has a strong following in the interior among the low classes, and with the prestige of a revolutionist back of him, may greatly influence the popular vote. It should be mentioned that minor elections had been held in a number of places, this city included, but which have been declared void.

With reference to the situation and in so far as American interests are concerned, I have to inform you that up to the present time this office has not been informed of any organized or concerted action on the part of the natives to imperil life or property. Fears have been expressed of a general uprising, but nothing has come of it. There is considerable unrest among the American colonists in this district, of whom many have returned home. Isolated cases of robbery committed by natives have happened among these people, but this, in my opinion, has no political significance and may be expected in any scantily settled and out of the way locality, where things run themselves and the nearest official may be removed ten miles from the place. When you consider that among these colonists there are but few who possess even a smattering of Spanish, differences and misunderstandings must arise, frequently culminating in threats of violence.

As to the distribution of State and Federal troops and rurales in this district, little can be said. The fact is that there are probably no more than 300 soldiers in this city at the present time. This number is increased by the sailors on naval vessels in this harbor to the number of 100 more. Small detachments of rurales and federal soldiers are being continually moved about in the interior from one place to another; the exact number of these cannot be determined, but do not exceed in all 500 men altogether, and frequently in parties of less than 50 men. The movements of these forces are never made public and usually take place at night; their destination is kept secret whenever possible to do so. As Veracruz is a home station for the Mexican gulf squadron, it happens that whenever troops are to be sent to Yucatan they are embarked here; but the number rarely exceeds 200 at a time, and these are usually transported there to take the place of others returning.

In the foregoing report I have endeavored to give a clear insight into existing conditions here at present, in the hope that I shall have no occasion to write up a more alarming state of affairs.

(signed) Wm. W. Canada
American Consul.

T E L E G R A M   R E C E I V E D

FROM: El Paso, Texas

Feb. 7, 1912

Rec'd 3:32 p.m.

Secretary of State,
    Washington.

Local authorities at Casas Grandes have declared against the Government. All officials including soldiers are in sympathy with the movement. Railroad communications between Juarez and that section abandoned. That portion of my district is reported to be wholly in the control of the anti-Madero followers. They are also making demonstrations against the Americans. They have made a demand of the people of the colonies (Mormons) to surrender their firearms (their private property). This demand the Americans will resist and serious trouble is feared. I will send a written protest to said local officials using to some extent the language of one year ago as given by the Ambassador.

Thos. D. Edwards

T E L E G R A M   R E C E I V E D

FROM: Mexico

Dated February 8, 1912.

Rec'd February 9, 1912,
2:40 a.m.

Secretary of State,
      Washington.

February 8, 10 p.m.

The following is the situation.

In the south the Federals have gained some small victories but Rebels have taken town of Chapala. Practical anarchy exists in the state of Michoacan and I am informed by unofficial sources that similar conditions prevail in Sinaloa and Sonora. In the north the Rebels have complete control of the state of Chihuahua and the Federal Government is helpless. Communication on the International Railway is interrupted by destruction of a bridge at San Pedro, Coahuila. Much anti-American sentiment in dangerous center of Torreon. In this city the unrest and apprehension grow. A petition to the permanent commission is being circulated among members of congress for an extraordinary session using the words "To save the country".

WILSON.

Mexico, February 8, 1912.

Serial 1254
File 54

The Honorable
    The Secretary of State,
        Washington.

Sir:

For the information of the Department I have the honor to transmit herewith a copy of a report on political conditions addressed to this Embassy by the American Consular Agent at Oaxaca, Mexico.

I have the honor to be,

Sir,

Your obedient servant,

(signed) Henry Lane Wilson

Enclosure:
    From Consular Agent Lawton, February 5, 1912.

AMERICAN CONSULAR SERVICE,

Oaxaca, Mexico.

February 5, 1912.

Honorable Henry Lane Wilson,

    American Ambassador,

        Mexico, D. F.

Sir:

I have to report that since formulating my report to you, of date January 29th, there have come to the surface here political conditions which were unsuspected. This is no doubt due to reports of rebellion on the northern frontier, but seems to be directed against the Secretario del Gobierno, Lic. Heliodora Diaz Quintas. Incidentally, Governor Juarez comes in for considerable condemnation, on account of failure to fulfill campaign promises, but as Quintax is recognized as the administrator of the Government policy (State) he is mostly condemned. A report has been circulated that tonight a manifestation will be made against him, and as his house is directly in front of the Consulate I visited the Governor and asked that care be taken to have no anti-foreign demonstration against the Consulate. The police have been advised and it is probable that no demonstration will take place.

A few days since a crowd of students paraded at night, in sympathy with the Argentine, Ugaret, in which the cry "Mueren los gringoes" was freely used. No other overt act was committed nor was any police action taken. I casually mentioned to the Jefe Politico that I thought it was very inopportune to allow such demonstrations without some sort of police surveillance. I will inform you of any other further political activity. I think it possible that sympathizers for the northern rebels may develop here.

I am, Sir,

Your obedient servant,

E. M. LAWTON,
American Consular Agent.

Mexico, February 12, 1912.

His Excellency Manuel Calero,
      Minister for Foreign Affairs.

Mr. Minister:

I am in receipt of urgent telegraphic instructions from the Department of State at Washington to call to Your Excellency's attention the fact that the anti-Madero insurgents at Casas Grandes, Chihuahua, are making hostile demonstrations against the Americans, especially the Mormon colonists, and at the same time demanding the surrender of their arms. My Government directs me to earnestly protest against the taking of firearms from Americans in disturbed districts in Mexico, either by federal forces or by revolutionists, it being clearly evident that they should not be left without protection or the means thereof from marauding robbers during the prevailing lawlessness in many sections of the Republic. While calling Your Excellency's attention to this situation in Casas Grandes and reserving all rights for future reclamations for injuries to the property or persons of American citizens, I must ask Your Excellency to be good enough to see that no obstacles are placed in the way of the Americans in any of the disordered districts to prevent their securing and possessing the arms and weapons necessary to the procurement of their bodily safety and the safety of their property. Your Excellency will permit me to observe that in the judgment of my Government a liberal policy in this direction will not only furnish Americans with the means of protecting themselves against the enemies of society but will inure to the benefit of the Mexican Government in that it will have the effect of reducing the number of calls for protection.

I avail myself of this occasion to renew to Your Excellency, the assurance of my high consideration.

HENRY LANE WILSON

W/pk

AMERICAN CONSULAR SERVICE

TO ALL AMERICAN CITIZENS RESIDING IN THIS
CONSULAR DISTRICT.

The Honorable PHILANDER C. KNOX, SECRETARY OF STATE, WASHINGTON, authorizes this Consulate to officially deny, through the local press and otherwise, all foolish stories of intervention, than which nothing could be further from the intentions of the Government of the United States, which is not concerned with Mexico's internal political affairs and which demands nothing but the respect and protection of American life and property.

The Government of the United States also requests that you will observe the strictest neutrality or impartiality and in no wise interfere between contending forces counselling your fellow countrymen to do likewise, and above all not to take part in nor discuss any political matters, for such action cannot but create animosity towards all American Citizens.

Enclosed you will find a number of circulars in Spanish, which you are requested to give the widest possible circulation, by posting and otherwise, to secure the object sought to be obtained.

WILLIAM W. CANADA,
American Consul.

Veracruz, Mex., February 13, 1912.

AMERICAN CONSULAR SERVICE

C. P. Diaz, Mexico

Feb. 13, 1912.

No. 440.

SUBJECT: Conditions on both sides of and near the line
separating America from Mexico.

The Honorable
    The Secretary of State,
        Washington, D. C.

Sir:

I have the honor to advise that according to reports brought into this City, the dissatisfied Maderists are still engaged in robbing Haciendas or Ranches not distant from Ciudad Porfirio Diaz, Mexico, and yesterday I was advised that they had burned the houses of two ranches within 60 miles of the City named, and a body of them had been seen very near this City. Inside the City of C. P. Diaz, the people apparently have little interest in the Madero Administration or the dissatisfied element that is going about the adjacent Country robbing and committing other depredations, and trains are arriving and departing irregularly.

Passengers on trains from the Laguna District of this State declare that the dissatisfied Maderists in that District are over 1,200 fairly well armed and munitioned men, and that they are proclaiming Senor Emilio Vasquez Gomez, now in San Antonio, Texas, for President of the Republic of Mexico. That said Rebels have demanded the surrender of the City of Torreon, but the Authorities still have confidence in the Maderists in the Garrison. That these Rebels have affected an organization and rob only when necessity compels them to do so. That they enter Towns, secure all they desire and then abandon them. That trains do not run regularly in and out of Torreon and only occasionally to and from C. P. Diaz. That few trains have recently been despatched to points South of Torreon. That quite frequently the telegraph lines are cut at points near Torreon. That farmhands have recently joined the dissatisfied Maderists and have assisted them in robbing the ranches in the State of Durango, and that the various Consuls in the City of Durango have asked for, through their Diplomatic Representative in the City of Mexico, Mexico, additional military protection.

It is evident that Senor Abram Gonzalez, Minister of the Interior of the Mexican Government and also Governor of the State of Chihuahua, Mexico, has finally succeeded in reaching the City of Chihuahua, and is in conference with the various Maderists Loyal Officials, but it is also evident that the dissatisfied Maderists, commanded by Antonio Rojas Ex-Maderist Col., and Braulio Hernandez Ex-Secretary of the State of Chihuahua, are still in the field, robbing ranches and people in that State. General Pascual Orozco seems to be, as yet, an uncertain quantity, as both the Loyal and dissatisfied Maderists allege that he is with them. It is the general opinion that he is for "Pascual Orozco" first and always.

The proclamation issued by the Governor of Chihuahua, on the 8th, instant, which in part reads:-

"The United States of America has declared that we are an inferior race, incapable of Self-Government, and unworthy to figure in the concert of free people, AND ARE PREPARING A FORMIDABLE ARMY TO INVADE AND PROFANE THE SACRED GROUND OF OUR BELOVED COUNTRY," has created considerable comment on both sides of the line separating America from Mexico, and has caused many Americans to fear that they will be molested by ignorant Mexicans, who do not understand such proclamations, that is for what purpose they are intended. To me it seems that the established Government, or rather the high Officials of the established Government, of Mexico, whenever they deem it convenient or necessary for the purpose of bringing all Mexicans to one

State of mind, take pleasure in flaunting "INTERVENTION BY THE UNITED STATES OF AMERICA," before the masses in Mexico.

Two carbons of this Despatch are enclosed, one will be sent to the Hon. Am. Ambassador to Mexico, Mexico City, Mexico, and another to the Hon. Am. Consul-General to Northern Mexico, Monterrey, Mexico.

I have the honor to be, Sir,

Your obedient servant,
(signed) Luther T. Ellsworth,
American Consul.

Enclosures:

2 carbons of this Despatch.

UNITED SUGAR COMPANIES
LOS MOCHIS, SINALOA,
MEXICO.

Los Mochis, February 15, 1912.

Hon. James R. Mann,
       House of Representatives,
            Washington, D. C.

Dear Mr. Mann:

It occurs to me that affairs in Mexico may be attracting attention and, as a correspondent on the spot, I would like to say to you that ever since my arrival, several weeks ago, conditions have been getting worse and are now very rapidly approaching a crisis. In fact, so far as this State is concerned, the crisis has already arrived.

Telegraphic connections have been cut in all directions. The railroad south is paralyzed because of burned bridges. Several haciendas and towns have been sacked and burned. Trains are being held up. The state officials are abandoning their posts in fear for their lives. Guerrilla bands are roaming all over the state, robbing and murdering. One of our neighboring plantations was held up the other day and all animals, arms and money taken. In fact we are in bad shape all around.

You will remember that last April I was in Washington on behalf of our interests here, asking for some sort of protection for the lives and properties of the American Colony here, the most populous one on the West Coast of Mexico, and having an investment of several millions of dollars of American capital. At that time I was turned down and the Americans here were left to take their chances.

At the present time the situation is worse, due largely to the fact that the present movement has no political basis but is purely one of pillage which the absence of a strong central government renders impossible of control.

Under these circumstances I again desire to appeal to our Government to send a gunboat of some kind to Topolobampo Bay, some twelve miles from here, so that at least the women and children of this community will have some chance of escaping with their lives.

Whatever may have been the reasons which impelled our Government to adopt the attitude it did last year, there can be no possible excuse for not sending a vessel into Topolobampo Bay at this time; in fact I am sure that, unofficially, the Mexican Government would welcome such action.

Now that I am here on the ground I realize more strongly than ever before the necessity of action by our Government and the justice of the demands of the colony here for the ordinary protection that all civilized nations give to their citizens. I tell you frankly that this business of "carrying the flag to extend United States commerce" is a rather disheartening process when one finds that its protection is refused at critical moments.

I want, if possible, to make one point clear, i.e. there will be no use sending the vessel after we have been burned out.

Very respectfully yours,
JAMES W. NYE.

FOR GOD'S SAKE SEE THAT THIS DOES NOT GET INTO THE NEWSPAPERS.

J.W.N.

T E L E G R A M   R E C E I V E D

> FROM: Mexico City
>
> DATED: Feb. 24, 1912
>
> REC'D: Feb. 25, 1912,
>   10:35 a.m.

Secretary of State,
    Washington, D. C.

        February 24, 9 p.m.

    URGENT. CONFIDENTIAL. Supplementing my telegram of February 24, 3 p.m., which was written under the pressure of the Department's urgency. I must suggest the wisdom of making it clear in any possible declaration relative to the crossing of the frontier at Ciudad Juarez that it is a part of Mexico in rebellion against the Federal Government and that our action is not unfriendly but friendly in character to the constituted authorities. I must further recommend that in case the action contemplated is taken that demonstrations in force be made on the frontier and that was vessels be immediately despatched to Guaymas, Mazatlan, Manzanillo, Acapulco and Salina Cruz and on the Atlantic to Tampico and Vera Cruz. A naval demonstration will be useful not only in impressing the Mexican mind but may also be useful in taking off American refugees. Americans in this City and throughout the Republic are generally armed and I think that it will be possible to organize a force of Americans and other foreigners in this City sufficient to afford protection and I shall immediately take steps in that direction when the Department's telegrams seem to indicate the necessity.

    Americans here generally believe that Ciudad Juarez will be taken without a contest but it should be well understood that if we cross the frontier line there the possibilities are that we shall ultimately have to go further.

Americans in Mexico will resent intervention which is not thorough and which will not secure them premanent guarantees. The Department should also consider the feasibility of instructing me to warn the Mexican Government against any contemplated action at Ciudad Juarez which might involve the loss of American lives in El Paso.

WILSON.

TELEGRAM SENT

DEPARTMENT OF STATE,
Washington

February 24, 1912.

Amembassy,

Mexico.

Urgent. Strictly confidential. The President desires reply within four hours. Paragraph.

The President feels that his duty and public opinion absolutely forbid toleration of any repetition of injury to Americans on American soil, as now threatened at Juarez, and he is disposed to give public warning that in such emergency he would be obliged to order troops to cross the line, as a police measure, and to disarm or drive away from Juarez any fighting forces threatening life in El Paso, thereafter returning.

Telegraph your judgment on this proposed action in reference to the safety of Americans in Mexico generally and also your judgment whether it is not now time to advise them to withdraw.

(signed) Huntington Wilson

T E L E G R A M   R E C E I V E D

FROM: Mexico

DATED: February 27, 1912

REC'D: February 28, 1912
         3:30 a.m.

Secretary of State,
    Washington.

    February 27, 10 p.m.

    Just received by circuitous route partly telephone and partly
telegraph a message from Consular Agent at Torreon. He reports
conditons throughout the Laguna district very critical with provisions
hardly sufficient for two weeks. Situation dangerous at mines and
haciendas which are now completely isolated. Says reports sent out by
Federal officials are garbled and untrue. More than fifteen hundred
foreigners in Torreon and no railway and infrequent telegraph service.
Says fifty-three Americans are holding the Velardena mining camp
against insurgents and have driven them off but expect them to return
in larger force and ask protection. I have made vigorous
representations and have advised the German Minister who is deeply
interested. In the state of Vera Cruz situation grows worse generally
and a band of insurgents estimated from a thousand to two thousand is
advancing from the south and having taken several towns is invading
the Tamaulipas and Vera Cruz oil district where millions of American
money are invested and a large American population resides.

    Have made representations.

                                        WILSON.

T E L E G R A M   R E C E I V E D

FROM: Mexico City,
        Mexico

DATED: February 29, 1912

REC'D: 9:00 P.M.

Secretary of State,
    Washington.

February 29, 3 p.m.

Department's February 28, 5 p.m. The action contemplated in question one would better be preceded by the action contemplated in question two. The tentative draft with reference to the latter is approved.

As to the probable effect of the action contemplated it cannot help lead to a very large emigration of American women and children to the United States, a movement which has already commenced from Mexico City and other points. It is probable that American men would withdraw from isolated points but not from large centers of population where they can find counsel and concerted action. Another result of the action would be to profoundly affect Mexican opinion and perhaps excite it. It might also have a somewhat depressing effect upon the Government. The wisdom of the policy should be inferred from the probable effects stated, with the added consideration that the situation seem to grow worse from day to day. It might be well in the instruction to authorize me to specifically name the localities from which I believe withdrawal should be made and to authorize consuls to take charge of the effects of our nationals. I know of no better course to follow than this; it is the only one left, eliminating intervention, which is not contemplated, and the closing of our diplomatic and consular establishments following a protest which is an even more extreme measure.

WILSON.

AMERICAN CONSULATE
Nuevo Laredo, Mexico

Despatch No. 161.   March 1, 1912.

SUBJECT: Danger to Americans in case of intervention.

The Honorable
    The Secretary of State,
        Washington, D. C.

Sir:

I have the honor to inform the Department that I have reliable information that during the Madero revolution the City of Mexico was divided up into seventy districts by an anti-American junta, and forty Mexicans were allotted to each district who were instructed in case of intervention at a given signal to attack all American residents of the district to which they were assigned. The attacks were to be made simultaneously and all Americans slain before they could have an opportunity to get together for defense.

The forty men in each district were supplied with diagrams showing the exact location of each American family, the number of persons in each family, the number of males in the family, and the probable amount of resistance which would be made.

The plan was in case of intervention to exterminate the American residents at one blow, and this plan probably extended to other cities in Mexico. That a similar feeling still exists is evident by an incident which occurred in Mexico City a few days ago.

An American whose complexion is rather dark, and who could easily be mistaken for a Mexican, was writing a message in the telegraph office in Mexico City, when two young Mexicans belonging to the better classes entered, and one of them said "I hope the Gringos will intervene, if they do won't we have fun killing Yankees". The other made a very cordial response and seemed to be in perfect accord with the views of his friend. I have this information direct from the gentleman who overheard the conversation.

This revolution is entirely without cause or principle and is being backed by politicians who were displaced by the former revolution and bandits who are ready to "Viva" for anybody so that they can have an excuse to pillage towns and ranches.

While Emilio Vasquez Gomez has proclaimed himself provisional President the masses of the Mexican people do not want him and his accession to the Presidency would only provoke a more determined revolution, in fact there is no one at present who could take the place of President Madero and restore order.

There is a feeling of insecurity here as the Mexican Government has sent the soldiers, with the exception of seventy-five infantry to other parts. The majority of the citizens here however are loyal to the Madero Government, and there is no fear of an uprising.

Any disturbance here must come from outside sources, but for its moral effect I think it advisable for the American Government to keep two or three hundred American soldiers at Fort McIntosh, Laredo, Texas.

I have the honor to be, sir,

> Your obedient servant,
> (signed) Alonzo B. Garrett
> American Consul.

AMERICAN CONSULATE

Mazatlan, Mexico

No. 145.   March 1st, 1912.

SUBJECT: Political Situation.

The Honorable,

    The Secretary of State,

        Washington, D. C.

Sir:

I have the honor to enclose account of outrages committed on American Citizens in the Culiacan Valley. Also a resume of the situation up to Feb. 28th., to which I have to add that a Mr. Tompkins, superintendent of a mine belonging to Mr. Beveridge, an American, near Cosala, was assaulted and at the point of a revolver deprived of his money, arms and all the powder at the mine; also of bar steel which they cut up in lengths for making of dynamite bombs.

Situation changes daily, at times for the better, again for the worse. It is difficult, if not impossible, to get reliable data, until it is too old to be of resource. I would state that (confidentially) that data as to number of Federal Troops, as in my No. 144, was given by the Lt. Col. of troops here. It appears to me to be an underestimate, there are probably some 10,000.

I have the honor to be, Sir,

                            Your obedient servant,
                            (signed) Wm. E. Alger
                            American Consul.

Enclosure

Outrages in Culiacan Valley

News of the present uprising in the Culiacan Valley came the 13th. inst. by telephone from Navolato and Las Trancas. A small number of men had ridden North from the vicinity of El Dorado and entered Navolato. They collected from the Mexican people there several hundred pesos in money and about an equal amount in value in goods and after some hours in possession retired to the North side of the Culiacan River. Their number was increased to about 80 from Navolato and was probably doubled again from the vicinity within the following two or three days.

In Navolato they did not molest Americans except that they took some horses and mules belonging to the Nelson Rhoades Sugar Co. which Mr. Lines, the manager induced them to return.

A day or two later most of this party moved Northwest across the Southern Pacific Railway into the foothills, burning a bridge as they passed.

The government acted with much energy, sending about 50 soldiers into Navolato the afternoon of the day that the rebels appeared there and subsequently patrolling the valley and driving them into the brush or to their homes. Also it sent a detachment speedily against the party that crossed to the Northwest, intercepting them about thirty-five miles up the railroad and beating quite a bunch of them, killing a few and taking about fifty-five horses and saddles. A smaller part of the rebels remained in the neighborhood of Navolato scattering in the outlying places and retiring to their homes.

Since the first few days the government has increased the number of its troops in the city and vicinity to severa hundred, I think they claim a thousand today. The rebels have also increased their numbers, being estimated all the way from 1000 to 2000, and they are pretty much in possession of the hills along the Easterly side of this District and that of Cosala and Badiraguato. It is reported that they have taken the town of Badiraguato, but it is impossible to know. It is also insisted that there is a fight on at Mocorito today which it is impossible to tell the truth of at the time of writing. The group of rebels who did not cross to the Northwest from Navolato seem to be in the brush and ranches between the Culiacan and the San Lorenzo rivers.

The government policing drives the gangs from the immediate vicinity. But the troops are for the most part from other states while the rebels belong to the neighborhood and have relations and friends at every hand. There is enough of actual insurrection to give parties who are nothing more than marauding gangs something of standing and partisans and where foreigners are concerned the patrolling of any particular property or protection to any people, sets the countryside against us. And while the insurrection lasts the retirement of the government patrols or detachments from any locality, will be followed by the reappearance of the local raiders and robbers.

The general feeling among the working people of the city about a week ago seemed to be growing steadily in favor of the new rebellion though not with the unanimity of the former revolution. Very many have had all the war that they want and are slow to cast in with the new movement. In the country I do not believe that the insurrection has spread with much heat or strength except in the mountains. The bulk of the people want to be let alone to follow their work, albeit that the belief seems to be general with them that justice and right is on the side of those dissatisfied with the outcome of the last revolution. The strength of the government in number and vigorous use of the troops has been very discouraging to the spirit of the revolt the past week in this valley.

Following is a statement of the violence against Americans from the appearance of the present insurrection to date, Feb. 13 – 28.:

Tuesday the 13th., Frank E. Doniwiler and wife and Charles Matlin were robbed at their farm about three miles Northwest from Navolato in the locality called El Boleon. Doniwiler was robbed in the last revolution and it is significant that at the first uprising of the revolution he was taken. The parties were at least in part local people. They took from him money, a clock, groceries and shot gun cartridges. In the house were Mr. and Mrs. Doniwiler and their baby and Charles Matlin. The party was rough and threatening but put no violence upon them than required for robbery.

Thursday 15th., Jacob Vetter and E. P. Fowler were robbed at their farm a little Northwest of Culiacancito. The robbers took the little money that they had and their arms. Mr. Vetter's wife was with him with their family of four or five small children. Mr. Vetter has now moved his family into Culiacan, but goes back and forth to the ranch every few days.

Friday the 16th., a small party of rebels went to the Yevabito ranch, about four miles East from Navolato owned by the Sinaloa Land Co. They demanded what arms might be there and also money. The arms were refused them but they were given a little money. Later in the day a small party returned demanding horses, Mr. Barbee who is in charge of the ranch refused them. A revolver was drawn on him, held close to him with threat to kill. He still refused to yield the horses however and they went away unsuccessful. There were quite a number of Americans living at this place, and at least one woman. All being settlers or employees of the Sinaloa Land Co. About half of these parties remain still, the balance having gone to the states.

Sunday morning the 18th., Mr. C. J. Stafford was robbed at the main ranch house of the Colorado Ranch which lies about two miles west from Culiacancito. Mr. Stafford was there alone. A band of about 25 appeared there just before daylight and knocked at his door saying "Open the door friend". He parlied [sic] with them declining to open. A shot was fired through the door. Still he refused and another shot was sent through the door; Mr. Stafford continuing to decline to open. He then heard them say bring the bomb, and a moment afterwards a piece of dynamite was exploded at the bottom of the door driving a hole through the door and sill. He then opened the door and they robbed him of his money and watch.

The Colorado Ranch has shortly been subdivided for colonization, one of the blocks being bought by Mr. John Jackson; his place being about a mile North of the ranch house in the brush, where he lives with his wife. Sunday morning the Jacksons were robbed. Five men going to their place and taking from them their arms and money. Later the same day or the next day they were robbed of household things, shoes, blankets and things of that kind. This last robbery was during the night and the robbers remained threatening and searching for about two hours. They demanded fifty pesos which Mr. Jackson did not have and so could not give them. From what he says he believes these last parties thought he was Coffee, who they were informed had these articles. The Jacksons are now in Culiacan.

The following day Ed Coffee, another settler of the Colorado Ranch, living about half a kilometer from Jackson was robbed of revolver and money.

And the day following that Mr. Chas. R. Bushnell, another settler on the Colorado Ranch living near Coffee and Jackson was robbed. The raiders taking his horses, some arms, money and household things. This same day Coffee was robbed again. He had one gun which was hidden. The robbers were informed about it and with revolver and saber flourish threatened to shoot him and spit him and hang him up by the neck. He yielded up the gun.

The 19th., the main Colorado Ranch was raided again for horses. They got some but just what I am not informed.

The 20th., or 21st., two horses were stolen from Mexican Cowboys of the Trancas Ranch, lying about five miles Southwest from Navolato.

Within the past few days the ranch of Mr. Orliff Shepardam has been robbed of considerable amounts of fuel wood which was cut and standing there. Other of such wood was burned and his fences burned. The burning was done at the same time with dry brush piled from clearing done some time since and whether the destruction of the fencing was intentional or not directly so, I do not know at the time of the writing.

This completes the list so far as I know and I think that up to this time that there are no more. The statements of the leaders at the time of the appearance of their bands near Navolato were that they were to treat the Americans exactly the same as in the other revolution. The failure to do so may be partly the result of the fact that these leaders went across the country into the foothills with the main following, leaving none behind who carried any degree of responsibility.

In an effort to read the meaning of these raids truly it should be observed that no bodily violence has been actually committed. Every kind of violence was threatened against Jackson and to less degree against Coffee, Bushnell and Doniwiler, but none carried out. Furthermore the things which were primarily the object of most of the robberies were arms, money and horses, things most essential to the rebels, and all of the Americans were known to have arms while the Mexican owners and people had none. At the beginning of the uprising two weeks ago and through the first days, notwithstanding the declaration of the leaders, there arose quite a strong anti-American feeling. This has subsided so far as relation to the revolt is concerned, except that the robberies against the Americans in the name of the Revolt, and then pursuit of the robbers by the government has in a way set those of the revolt against us. There is always present anti-American sentiment because of the apprehension of intervention, which is another matter, but even this is growing to be of "Old Sore" effect. So long as the move does not take place.

I have forgotten to state that Feb. 14th., or 15th., an American was robbed at El Dorado and lawlessness was so in possession that the four or five Americans there, employees of the sugar factory of the Redo Co., came out and went to the states. All men.

The 16th., about half the women and children were sent out to the States from Culiacan and vicinity.

The Government has a large force of troops and Rurales here now, but it is an immense task to police all the country, and the rebels or simple robbers as the case may be are among their relatives and friends.

The situation is not so acute as ten days ago, but still contains all the elements for swift trouble any hour. The killing of somebody, which is likely to occur at any of those raids, would be certain to turn the whole population upon us. Up to now there has been a long seated restraint and fear of the consequences upon the people relative to the abuse of any American, but the successful and unpunished raids have lost us this, in fact contempt is swiftly taking its place, and the raiders are becoming more bold and insolent. Every robbery is a distinct loss to the whole situation.

To meet this we have got to gather in a few places where arms are carried openly and where there is enough show of strength to discourage any more robbers. At Mr. Shepley's Ranch of Palos Blancos are about eight men. This place is about nine miles North of Culiacan on the Humaya River.

At the Vardugo Ranch about four miles East of Navolato, on the North side of the river are about ten men, three women and some children. At neither of these places will they submit to being robbed. At Verdugo now are Coffee and Bushnell.

At the Yevabito Ranch are quite a number. Also at the Trancas ranch are two or three. At Navolato there are fifteen or more Americans with several women and children. And here in Culiacan probably now fifteen or twenty men and a few women.

In case of any general descent upon us, through the result of violence offered and resisted, or because of intervention of some kind

of armed incoming of United States forces, we would have to go out if
we could. If the railroad should be cut at the time, our only way will
be to get together as quickly as we can and go down the Valley to
make a stand at Atlanta or somewhere this side until we can be taken
care of by boat by our people.

In the meantime, the condition is really intolerable. We are trying
to make something out of this country and this means primarily the
farms at the beginning, and settlers. Many of these have crops on land
that has never been planted before since time began. They are driven
off.

* * * * * * *

DISTURBANCES IN MEXICO
****
By the President of the United States

A PROCLAMATION

WHEREAS serious disturbances and forcible resistance to the authorities of the established Government exist in certain portions of Mexico; and

WHEREAS under these conditions it is the duty of all persons within the jurisdiction of the United States to refrain from the commission of acts prohibited by the law thereto relating and subversive of the tranquillity of a country with which the United States is at peace; and

WHEREAS the laws of the United States prohibit under such circumstances all persons within and subject to their jurisdiction from taking part contrary to said laws in any such disturbances adversely to such established government; and

WHEREAS by express enactment if two or more persons conspire to commit an offense against the United States, any act of one conspirator to effect the object of such conspiracy renders all the conspirators liable to fine and imprisonment; and

WHEREAS there is reason to believe that citizens of the United States and others within their jurisdiction fail to apprehend the meaning and operation of the applicable laws of the United States as authoritatively interpreted and may be misled into participation in transactions which are violations of said laws and which will render them liable to the severe penalties provided for such violations;

NOW, THEREFORE, in recognition of the laws governing and controlling in such matters as well as in discharge of the obligations of the United States towards a friendly country, and as a measure of precaution, and to the end that citizens of the United States and all others within their jurisdiction may be deterred from subjecting themselves to legal forfeitures and penalties;

I, WILLIAM HOWARD TAFT, President of the United States of America, do hereby admonish all such citizens and other persons to abstain from every violation of the laws hereinbefore referred to, and to hereby warn them that all violations of such laws will be rigorously prosecuted; and I do hereby enjoin upon all officers of the United States charged with the execution of such laws the utmost diligence in preventing violations thereof and in bringing to trial and punishment any offenders against the same; and finally I do hereby give notice that all persons owing allegiance to the United States who may take part in the disturbances now existing in Mexico, unless in the necessary defense of their persons or property, or who shall otherwise engage in acts subversive of the tranquillity of that country, will do so at their peril and that they can in no wise obtain any protection from the Government of the United States against the appropriate legal consequences of their acts, in so far as such consequences are in accord with equitable justice and humanity and the enlightened principles of international law.

IN TESTIMONY WHEREOF, I have hereunto set my hand and caused the seal of the United States to be affixed.

DONE at the City of Washington this 2nd day of March, in the year of our Lord one thousand nine hundred and twelve, and of the Independence of the United States of America the one hundred and thirty-sixth.

WM. H. TAFT

T E L E G R A M   R E C E I V E D

> FROM: Mexico City
>
> DATED: March 4, 1912
>
> REC'D: March 5, 1912
>   2:30 a.m.

Secretary of State,
    Washington.

March 4, 10 p.m.

The Mexican Government has been fully advised in the sense of the Department's March 2, 3 p.m. and I have also communicated a copy of my notice of March three, nineteen hundred and twelve. The Mexican Government understands and appreciates in its right sense the President's proclamation and has authoritatively said so in the press. Unfortunately there are many foolish Mexicans and Americans who construe the proclamation wrongfully and these misconceptions I an endeavoring to correct. A very large emigration of American women and children from Mexico City is taking place due to malicious rumors and publications that Mrs. Wilson was leaving Mexico. This also I am endeavoring to correct. The news throughout the country is not reassuring but I avoid details because of confusion and the inability to carefully study the situation on account of the number of people invading the Embassy and demanding counsel.

                                    WILSON

Law Offices
HAFF, MESERVEY, GERMAN & MICHAELS
Suite 906, Commerce Building
Kansas City, Mo.

March 4, 1912

The President,
    White House,
        Washington, D.C.

Sir:

I take the liberty of enclosing herewith confirmation of the telegram which I sent to your Excellency last evening. The telegram may appear to you somewhat earnest, but I sincerely hope it will not be considered as a criticism. I feel it my duty because of my intimate knowledge of the conditions in Mexico to express to you my opinion, and not only that, but to assure you that what I say represents the opinion of those Americans who have something to lose in Mexico.

If you will but one moment reflect, you will see how impossible it is to consider consular protection. How, for instance, the consul at Hermosillo, Sonora, without even a clerk, could be expected at one moment to protect twenty million dollars worth of property owned by the Montezuma Copper Company at Nacozari, Sonora, of which I am the legal representative, distant two hundred and fifty miles across the mountains from the home of the consulate.

Its properties consist of concentrators, smelters, mines, locomotives, one hundred and thirty kilometers of railroad and all its equipment and buildings, consisting of houses, stores, warehouses, shops, and the personal property of five thousand employees and large stocks of merchandise and stores and large quantities of ores and other properties too numerous to mention, of which the consul could not even have knowledge, much less take an inventory which would be necessary in making any reclamation against the Mexican Government, in case of destruction of those properties. At the same time, this consul would be expected to protect the property of the Tiger Mining Company; valued as six millions of dollars and located one hundred miles further in the mountains of Sonora, and consisting of stamp mills, cyanide plants, store buildings, houses, mining machinery of every kind, too numerous to mention, and in the very opposite direction from Hermosillo would be located some half dozen other American enterprises of like character, including Promontorio Mines, the Giroux Mining Company, the mines and smelters of the San Antonio Copper Company, great properties of the Cananea Consolidated Copper Company at Cananea, Sonora, valued at fifty million of dollars, covering more than twenty thousand acres and involving smelters, concentrators, railroads and railroad property and the houses and buildings taking care of a population of some twenty five thousand people, all of whom get their living working for this mining company.

We need not go further with the illustration to convince you that Americans residing in Mexico cannot abandon their interests there, and that any such advice as that only serves to stir up trouble for them in Mexico by exciting the disgust of Mexicans who are put in position of being declared either unable or unwilling to extend the protection which their position as a civilized nation requires them to give to foreign investments.

I have already, in a previous communication of the 6th of February, called your attention to the delicacy of the situation and to the well defined effort of a large class of Americans residing in the border cities of the United States to cause trouble and to agitate intervention, which is altogether to be deprecated and discouraged in the best interests of American citizens residing in Mexico and in the best interests of the future friendly relations of the United States with all Latin American countries.

All who advocate American intervention, or interference in Mexico, are either badly informed of the true interests of Americans in that country, or else are politically ambitious and strangely indifferent to the welfare of American citizens and to the good name of the United States and the reputation of your worthy administration.

I am enclosing you herewith an interview in today's associated press dispatch with Lic. Vera Estanol, late Minister of Public Instruction and Gobernacion (Interior) in the cabinet of Ex-President Diaz. This will, I am sure, be very instructive to you and your Secretary of State, as they have been to the American people who have read them. From this interview with Sr. Vera Estanol, published today, you will understand better the problems with which the Mexican Government has to deal and you will better understand the problems which would be inflicted upon the United States (impossible of solution) if we should be injudicious enough to intervene in that country's affairs.

You may rely upon the wisdom and the correctness of these statements of Lic. Vera Estanol. I know him intimately. He is the practical leader of the most intelligent classes of Mexico today and he accepted the invitation from the Kansas City Bar Association to address that association largely from a desire to do some missionary work in behalf of his country within the borders of the United States.

Trusting that you will pardon the length of this communication and that it will be at least suggestive, if not instructive, I beg to remain, Sir,

Your obedient servant,
(signed) Delbert James Haff

[Editor's note: Telegram referred to in above text not included.]

KANSAS CITY TIMES
MONDAY, MARCH 4, 1912.

"AMERICANS NEED NOT FLEE"
****
Senor Vera Estanol Says Taft's Advice Was Unnecessary.
****
Mexicans Will Respect Foreigners, the
Minister Under Diaz Believes--
Education Is Necessary to Calm
the People, He Explains.
****

That there is no necessity for the order given by President Taft
to Ambassador Wilson to advise Americans to leave Mexico on account of
the revolutionary troubles there, is the opinion expressed in Kansas
City last night by Jorge Vera Estanol, formerly minister of education
under President Diaz.

Senor Vera says Americans in Mexico are safe and that the only
effect of the order will be to spread needless alarm.

"Not wishing to criticise the action of the American government,"
he said, "I must differ with those who appear to believe Americans and
American interests are endangered in Mexico. Not at any time have they
been endangered. Federals and rebels alike have done all they could to
see that American rights were not trampled on.

"The effect of the order will, I believe, be very slight. Americans
have a billion dollars represented in various enterprises in Mexico and
there are thousands of citizens of the United States with their families
employed there. It is extremely unlikely that many of these will lay
down everything and leave."

The following statement of conditions in Mexico was given to the Associated Press here last night by Senor Vera, who spoke before the bar association recently:

Due to the last political disturbances which unfortunately have occurred in the republic of Mexico some more or less bitter comments have been made in the United States with regard to the situation. Those generally have not been based on a thorough knowledge of the facts and antecedents, and I desire as a tribute to truth and patriotism to explain those antecedents:

Mexico, when it obtained independence, had three vital problems--the economical, the social or educational and the political.

With regard to the economical problem: At that time all the landed property, which then constituted almost the only wealth of the country, was in dead hands, as follows: Two-thirds owned by ecclesiastic bodies and one-third, a small part of which represented Indian reservations, belonged to the heirs of the conquerors, who had adjudicated themselves immense tracts.

A country cannot prosper under such economical conditions. On that account our first steps after the independence of Mexico tended to free the property. The struggle absorbed all the political activity of Mexico, as the ecclesiastic bodies, especially the Roman Catholic Church, defended themselves, causing the civil war. These struggles lasted for fifty years. At their end was definitely established the principle of individual property in the Mexican republic as the foundation of its new economical organization.

But it was not only necessary to re-establish individual property, it was also necessary to develop, to work and to mobilize it.

The government of General Diaz from 1876 to 1910 devoted all its fundamental energies to secure the material government of the country, the investigation of its sources of wealth, their exploitation, the investment of capital. As a result the private corporations and the government won an enviable credit in Europe. The Mexican securities were firmly quoted in the Old World.

That explains that only in a secondary manner the Mexican government could devote part of its energies to the social and educational problem and to the political preparation of the Mexican nation for a genuine democratic government.

Without money it is impossible to promote public education, and without education a free country is impossible.

During the last years of the government of General Diaz efforts were made to promote public education. But it shall be taken into account that the Indian population represents 9 millions of inhabitants against less than 6 millions of white or mixed population, and also that some years ago 87 per cent of the population of the republic did not know how to read and write.

Consequently the superior classes have to carry out two colossal tasks--to impel the progress of the republic at a great speed in order to make it enter into the family of civilized nations, and to transform, little by little, an ignorant race into an active element of the community. Just think of the task of the leading classes in moving such a considerable dead weight as that of the passive classes!

We had lived during the Spanish government for more than three centuries under the rigid principle of authority, in our ideas, in our religion, in our politics, etc. A people cannot suddenly turn this secular mode of living into a free government; it has to do it by degrees.

That explains the present situation of the republic. The full citizenship having been granted to the whole nation, without distinction of the culture of its members, and the birth of the democratic government having been announced, the superior classes have understood that this means civil liberty, liberty within the order of things, but the ignorant classes have understood that this means license, liberty in disorder. They are not ruled by force, they are not guided by the discipline of education.

This is what is happening in Mexico; but this ought not to cause lack of confidence in the ultimate fate of the country, nor give way to bitter criticism of its public men; for after the effervescent moment has gone by, the directing classes, who are highly cultured and educated; the influential classes that have governed the Mexican republic ninety years with the greatest difficulties and enormous obstructions, but always successfully, will take hold anew of the situation, will dominate the disorderly element, and through a gradual process of civil and educational education, will ultimately allow the orderly exercise of citizenship, which will avoid new uprisings and revolutions. The same qualities of energy, patriotism and prudence which said ruling classes show in resolving the economic problem, considered as insolvent, which have also proved in making the program for the education of our Indian masses, will help them in carrying out with success the general plan of reorganization of the disorderly element of the country and in that of progressive education in the political ideals of liberty and democracy.

The re-establishment of order is sure, and once it has been attained, the country will start anew through is [sic] peaceful way, developing all its wealth.

****

THE KANSAS CITY JOURNAL,
THURSDAY, FEBRUARY 29, 1912.

"DIAZ OVERTHROWN BY FEW AMERICANS"
****

Senor Vera Estanol Here to Lecture,
Says Madero Tried to Stop.
****

JUAREZ FALL MISTAKE
****

Soldiers of Fortune Seized City Despite
Protests of Rebel Chief.
****

PEACE WAS NEAR ONCE
****

Revolutionary Spirit Now Is General
and the End Is Uncertain.
****

"A small thing sometimes may change the destiny of a government, make or break an empire or throw a republic into a state of anarchy. Had it not been for a few American soldiers of fortune, Diaz still would be president of Mexico, a reform cabinet would be in control and peace would reign throughout that now turbulent republic."

So said Senor Jorge Vera Estanol, a former member of the Diaz cabinet, who is here from the City of Mexico and will address the Bar Association tonight on "Equity and Law in the United States and Mexico." Senor Vera Estanol is the leader in Mexico of the popular evolutionist party and, though for a time in the Diaz cabinet, believes that the people should uphold the hands of President Madero, or any one else who may be president of the republic. He is a strong believer in law and order and says only anarchy and a reign of lawlessness can result from any revolution.

"The first fall of Juarez," Senor Vera Estanol said last night at the home of D. J. Haff, where he is being entertained, "was purely an accident, a serious mistake, brought on by a few soldiers of fortune. It is well known in Mexico that a few Americans with the revolutionary forces provoked the attack, and when it once got under way the revolutionists fell in behind them. General Madero tried to prevent it. Knowing of an agreement to the contrary, citizens of Juarez telephoned Madero at his camp outside the city. His reply was that he was ordering the attack to stop, even to demanding that the leaders be shot. But it was too late, and there was no discipline among his forces.

ONE DAY MEANT PEACE.

"Had that battle been delayed one day Madero would have been on his way to Mexico City and peace would have followed in the republic. It is a matter of public record in Mexico that Diaz had agreed to adopt the reforms advocated by the then revolutionists. These were effective suffrage, no re-election, better distribution of lands, reform in taxation, and reforms in the administration of justice. A personal representative of President Diaz, Senor Carbayal, went as a special envoy to Madero's camp with this new declaration or manifesto. As the revolutionists were conceded virtually everything General Madero agreed to cease hostilities and lay down arms.

"All of this was made public in Mexico and the attack on Juarez today is regarded as one of the most unfortunate epochs in the history of the republic. After Juarez was taken the victors would be satisfied with nothing but the resignation of President Diaz, and the complete overthrow of his government.

"Now all peace loving people are seeing that the action of the last cabinet after all was the wisest, because it would have prevented the mushroom growth of the revolutionary spirit which prevails. Now no one can foresee the ultimate end.

REVOLUTION AND ANARCHY.

"My position always has been to attack revolution as a method of getting political reforms, because revolution kills incipient democracy rather than encouraging and promoting it. Revolution leads to anarchy and anarchy, to be suppressed, requires despotic methods."

Senor Vera Estanol spoke of the provisional government, pending the election of Madero, while Francisco L. de la Barra was chief executive. He was there about five months when Madero went in after the election last October.

There is another matter which is of public record, the Mexican advocate said. Foreseeing the danger of holding an election while the revolutionary spirit still was rampant, the popular evolutionist party, through Senor Vera Estanol, as its leader, petitioned congress to postpone the election three or four months. It was desired, the petition stated, that the country be entirely peaceful and order restored so as to hold the first fair election under normal conditions.

"Madero sent a message to congress, almost menacing in its meaning, saying that if the election were postponed he would not be responsible for the actions of the people. The election then was ordered at once," the senor said.

INTERVENTION, WAR.

After speaking of some of the mistakes President Madero has made, such as ante-election promises, which were not carried out and mainly are responsible for the crisis in Mexico now, he was asked for an expression on the question of intervention by the United States.

"The Mexicans never will tolerate intervention," he said. "Such a move would serve to defeat the very end at which it is aimed.

Intervention would cause general bad feeling and war might be the
result."

The Mexican advocate said he was a member of the Diaz cabinet
but a short time, serving part of the time as minister of public
instruction and later as the head of the interior department. His idea in
accepting these portfolios, he said, was, if possible, to influence Diaz
to adopt a more liberal policy in order to satisfy the people.

****

THE KANSAS CITY STAR
WEDNESDAY, FEBRUARY 28, 1912

"MADERO PLEDGED TOO MUCH"
****
Broken Promises May Break the President,
Vera Estanol Says.
****
The Bar Association Speaker Supports the Government,
but Admits the Grievances of the Revolutionists-
Warns the United States.
****

The troubles in Mexico furnish a good example of the result of a president not keeping his platform promises, according to Senor Vera Estanol, who is to be a speaker before the bar association tomorrow night. From which it may be inferred that the senor is a progressive in his home politics. He is a progressive, but at the same time he feels that the part of every advocate of law and order in Mexico should be to support the government of Madero in the present crisis.

Mr. Vera was minister of public instruction in the last cabinet of President Diaz, and also acted as minister of the interior. He took a prominent part in the establishment of the provisional government after Diaz left the country and speaks of the present situation from intimate knowledge.

STANDS BY MADERO.

"No Mexican who has the welfare of his country at heart can do otherwise than oppose the action of the leaders who are trying to inaugurate a new revolution," Mr. Vera said at the Hotel Baltimore this morning. "At the same time it must be candidly admitted that President Madero has given much cause for dissatisfaction and by his rash and unstatesmanlike promises has armed the leaders of the present movement with effective arguments to stir up the ignorant and restless portion of the population. At the time of the former uprising Madero made the usual bid of revolutionary leaders for the support of the laboring classes by promising better wages and a division of the land. That is about all that is necessary to induce those classes to take up arms at any time and under any leader. These promises are now returning upon his head, and added to his other mistakes furnish the cause of the crisis that is threatening his government.

GAVE OFFICES TO RELATIVES.

"Another mistake was the breaking of the agreement whereby Francisco Vasquez Gomez was to have been elected vice-president on the ticket with Madero. He was displaced by Jose Pinto Suarez and this breach of good faith alienated the revolutionary leaders. In the formation of the government and the distribution of the offices Madero continued the same mistaken policy. He bestowed upon his relatives and favorites the rewards that the men who had made the revolution a success fancied belonged to them. The result has been that in the present crisis the old revolutionary leaders are against the government and Madero is forced to look for support to the very class that formerly was against him.

"The new movement, I should say, is almost wholly Socialistic in its nature. The masses who have no more understanding of the situation than is given them by their leaders in a few popular catch phrases like 'higher wages' and 'division of the land,' are being used by adroit politicians and generals as mere pawns in a game of which they, the leaders, will be the only ones to profit by if they succeed. With the people, therefore, the movement is socialistic, but with the leaders it is political. That has been the history of most uprisings in Mexico."

WOULD RESTRICT SUFFRAGE.

The remedy for the unstable condition of affairs in Mexico, Mr. Vera believes, lies in popular education, and until education is more general he would restrict the suffrage.

"What Mexico needs is extensive and not intensive education," he said. "It would be better that everybody should be able to read, write and count than that a few should be highly educated. Until our educational system can be placed upon this broader basis I would limit the suffrage so as to bar the ignorant and turbulent classes which have always been the disturbing factor in Mexican politics."

WARNS AGAINST INTERVENTION.

On one point Mr. Vera was positive and vehement. He declared that any intervention on the part of the United States would be most unfortunate and disastrous, and would inevitably mean war.

"Any Mexican government that should consent to the occupation of a foot of Mexican soil by any foreign power would be instantly torn to pieces," he said. "The United States, I hope, will never take so ill advised a step. American lives and property would not be safe and it would be impossible to foretell the end of all the evil consequences that would follow. The intelligent Mexicans who now are striving for a stable government, for law and order and the protection of property and credit would be wholly unable to control the situation if American troops once crossed the border."

Mr. Vera is to address the Bar Association tomorrow night on a purely legal subject. He will speak on the topic, "Equity and Law in the United States and Mexico." While in the city he will be a guest of D. J. Haff.

****

T E L E G R A M   R E C E I V E D

FROM: Mexico City

DATED: March 7, 1912

REC'D: March 8, 1912
         1:22 a.m.

Secretary of State,
    Washington.

March 7, 10 p.m.

The press reports the taking of Victoria, the capital of
Tamaulipas, which indicates what was reported in my cipher telegram
February 7, 10 p.m. that an arrangement exists among all the border
states with possibly the exception of Sonora. There are renewed
outbreaks in the State of Jalisco and some towns have been taken.
Miranda, a prominent general in the Madero revolution, has risen
against the Government in the State of Mexico near Xochimilco and is
reported to have a large force under his command. There are also
armed bands on the other side of Mexico State near Tumpango.
Outbreaks continue in the States of Vera Cruz, Puebla, Tlaxcala,
Oaxaca and Zacatecas. There are rumors tonight of radical changes in
the President's cabinet which if correctly stated are for the worse. The
American colony in Mexico City held a meeting today and appointed a
committee to act in conjunction with the committees of other colonies for
the protection of foreign interests. As the local authorities have advised
all foreigners to arm for protection and as the Governor of the Federal
district has advised me of his willingness to arm the foreigners and as
other diplomatic representatives are attending the meetings of their
nationals, I deemed it my duty to be present and during the meeting
which was attended by from five hundred to a thousand men, I
counselled all Americans to a strict observance of the law, obedience to
local authorities, avoidance of participation in Mexican politics and to

tender their services to the local government solely in the interest of law and order and for the protection of life and property. This rule will be strictly observed by all foreigners. I think it advisable that the Department should advise me exactly what my course should be in this situation as I do not desire to transgress any established precedents but simply to be an aid to our distressed nationals.

WILSON

AMERICAN EMBASSY
MEXICO

March 12, 1912.

Serial No. 1303
File No. 10y

The Honorable
    The Secretary of State,
        Washington.

Sir:

I have the honor to transmit herewith copy in translation of an article published in "El Imparcial", of this city, by Toribio Esquivel Obregon, a politician of some prominence at the present time, and who was one of the peace commissioners of the Diaz Government who conferred with Madero at Ciudad Juarez during the political disturbances of a year ago.

I have the honor to be,
Sir,
Your obedient servant,
(signed) Henry Lane Wilson

Enclosure: as stated.

Enclosure in No. 1303 (Translation). From "El Imparcial", City of Mexico, D. F., March 10, 1912.

IN FACE OF THE ENEMY.

There is a very dark, sinister point in our political situation, a dark point seen by everyone, but one which everyone dislikes to look upon prompted by a desire to deceive themselves in an effort to believe that the shadow will not invade us, that the horrors of a social disturbance will not end in a general agitation.

This dark point is in the attitude of the United States in view of the present conditions of Mexico.

The press in dealing with this very delicate matter, fearing that it has not sufficient data, has left its solution to the chancelleries and trusts in their action to solve the conflict, and the people, in view of the silence of the press, act also with levity in spite of the seriousness of the situation; it seems that though it has eyes it does not see, that while it has ears it does not hear.

I consider it a patriotic act to remove the veil with which the words of diplomacy may blindfold us, to the end that we may all be alive to the facts and assume a courageous attitude before them; not for the purpose of creating any alarm and excite any passions, but to avert the evil, to stop all rancor, in order that cool reflection may guide our steps.

It seems that there is an effort to deceive us with friendly words; it appears to me that there is an intention to keep us in confident indifference to the fact that we are destroying our own selves, weakening our strength and fostering hatred against each other in order that the prey may be easier and surer.

Under such conditions, the only thing that may lead us to union, the only thing that will permit us to know which Mexicans are capable of sacrificing everything and to see in their enemy of yesterday an ally and a brother, when the time comes to defend national honor and integrity, will be the consciousness of danger.

During the civil war that has been raging among us for over one year and a half, many foreigners who came here during our times of prosperity have suffered. Perhaps among all of them, those who have done the least to identify themselves with us have been the Americans, and perhaps they are also those who have suffered the least in their persons and property on account of the disturbance.

Americans have given shelter to the leaders of our revolutions, have contributed to them with arms and ammunition, have encouraged them with their approval and have lent the contingent of their men to hasten the success of such revolutions. Therefore, they are our co-partners in our responsibilities and honestly speaking they have nothing to complain about a situation created with their assistance and perhaps inspired by them.

The other foreigners, with very few exceptions, have conducted themselves in strict neutrality; and notwithstanding the fact that the Americans have suffered less and have contributed the most to cause this disturbance, they are the ones who menace us, they are the only ones who have armed their troops which cannot have other purpose than to take action against Mexico, and, finally, in the belief that the propitious moment has come, they are the ones who advise their fellow-citizens to leave the territory of Mexico, something which is only done a few days before a declaration of war.

But still we are lulled by words of sweetness; we are still told that those troops have no other purpose than to enforce neutrality, while our Consul is officially told that no order will be given to prevent the importation of arms into Ciudad Juarez, and when the rebels being in possession of this city, and there is no danger of any attack on other frontier towns, what can be the necessity of a display of force?

The exodus of Americans from our country, unhurt and without the least manifestation of hostility, is an evident proof that they are running no risk here any more than the rest of us, unless they do something to provoke us, either through their own acts or those of their government; therefore the attitude of the latter shows that its distrust and hostility obey a predetermined plan and that it is our duty to be on the alert and to evade at all cost the danger by which we are menaced. Let us not be deceived foolishly by words and protests of friendship which are not in accord with the facts. Let us remember our history in the case of the separation of Texas; the separation of Panama and Cuba's case, and if we are unfortunately engaged in a bloody encounter, let us not be haunted by the remorse of having been visionary and to give our enemy the opportunity to laugh at our credulity.

Let us do everything we can to avert the conflict. The people and the government should tend to this end and they should both rally under the same flag, the flag of our country.

Then all the civilized nations will have nothing to reproach us with, and then we shall fear no one.

If there is anything which will unite all Mexicans and which will undoubtedly uniform their purpose will be this cry which will find echo in every heart: IN FACE OF THE ENEMY.

One of the causes which has influenced the present revolution, is the idea of Mr. Madero that the government is his own and that he should make use of his authority and prestige in favor of his personal friends and to reduce to nothing those who will not submit to him easily.

This is the reason why, because Madero thinks that the Government is his own, the people do not look upon it as a national government, and it is essential that it should be, at all cost, and that President Madero should set aside his personal affections, to the end

that all of his acts may become really the acts of the President of the
Republic, to find his inspiration in the desires of the people, calling to
his assistance men who may be a guarantee to the nation.

The opposition party should have organized and uniformed public
opinion before resorting to arms, and only do this when the people
would have become convinced that the Government would not listen to
its demands.

                                        T. Esquivel Obregon.

AMERICAN CONSULATE
Tampico, Mexico

No. 475.   March 17, 1912

SUBJECT: Political Conditions in City of Tampico.

The Honorable
    The Secretary of State,
        Washington.

Sir:

Referring to despatch number 473 of the 16th, inst. I have the honor to advise the Department that the 16th passed without any attempt whatever at a demonstration against Americans as threatened in the anonymous letter. However, the Presidente Municipal received an anonymous letter stating that he was partly responsible for the American invasion and protection of the Americans and that he and his secretary would be killed. While these anonymous letters are not openly regarded seriously it is certain that the local authorities have been worried for several days and they have prepared as much as possible for emergencies. During the night of the fifteenth the gun boat <u>Bravo</u> kept the search light constantly on the city.

Judge H. T. McCabe, Editor of the <u>Tampico Times</u>, has received various several telegrams from President Madero and Francisco Azcena in regard to the situation. I have seen two of these telegrams and one of them speaks of certain letters of instructions being sent. The Federal Government evidently wished to get at the truth of the reports evidently published in the newspapers of the 16th, in regard to riots in Tampico.

That some parties are interested in fomenting, in an insidious manner, anti-American sentiment, is indicated by the publication in a local newspaper issued last night of an article entitled "El enimigo al frente"-(The enemy in front"). This is clearly directed against the United States but like the Anti-American Political circular reported in despatch 471 of the 14th, inst. and entitled "The Secret of Vasquez Gomez" it is written in such a manner as to make it difficult to allege that it is directed against Americans. Both of these articles profess to be political but their contents are calculated to arouse feeling against Americans. A copy of this article is herewith enclosed. This publication is under direction of Sam. Kelly and Julio Carroon whose names purported to be signed to the anonymous letter received at this office and men who are in control of the stevedores union. The attorney for the Union is Lic. Alba de Ramirez. These men have always been connected with political disturbances in Tampico. Kelly was one of the men who were arrested for trouble following the Gubernatorial election. With yesterdays issue of the paper was distributed another circular directed against Matias Guerra, the candidate who was declared elected and who was protested against by Kelly and his associates. In spite of his name Kelly is a Mexican and a Mexican citizen.

I have the honor to be, Sir,

Your obedient servant,
(signed) Clarence Arkell
American Consul.

[Editor's note: Article mentioned here is same as enclosed in previous section.]

CONFIDENTIAL

                                    Mexico, March 20, 1912.

Serial 1320
File 9y

The Honorable
    The Secretary of State,
        Washington.

My dear Mr. Knox:

Since the date of my confidential despatch of February 20, 1912, the area of revolution and disorder has materially increased in some parts of the Republic and decreased in others. On the whole I think the Government's position is less secure and its authority more restricted than they were a month ago. Since that time the State of Chihuahua has passed entirely out of the control of the Government; a new state organization has been created there and from within its territories a militant force has been recruited, with the sympathy and assistance of adjoining States, to march upon the Capital of the Republic. Whether this army from Northern Mexico will ever make much headway in its journey to the South may be doubted but it will probably be able to retain control of the State of Chihuahua and perhaps ultimately of the State of Sonora and remain a menace and a threat to the existence of the present Government of the Republic. By a superhuman effort the Government was able to organize and send to Torreon a force of about three thousand men. Otherwise it is very probable that at this moment the States of Durango and Coahuila would have made common cause with the State of Chihuahua and that Orozco would now be in control of two-thirds of the northern belt of States. Nor is it improbable that this event will yet come about through the increasing adverse sentiment against Madero's Government in the North, aided by political dissensions here, defective administrative methods, and the inefficiency of the army. On the other hand it is possible that the forces of Orozco, now supposed to be maintained by money and supplies from "cientifico" sources, may become discouraged and dissipated and that the Government may achieve negative victories through the lack of discipline or of a common purpose among its opponents.

Coming South from these border States, which with the exception of the State of Nuevo Leon are all affected by the revolutionary movement, we find in the States of Guanajuato, Zacatecas and Aguascalientes many disorders and in some parts a strong revolutionary movement, the States of San Luis Potosi, Queretaro, Hidalgo and Jalisco remaining comparatively calm, though isolated brigandage and lawlessness prove the lack of restraint and the inability of the Government to exert a positive and general respect for its authority. This description practically brings us to the State of Mexico and the South, South-Eastern and South-Western States, stretching to the Isthmus of Tehuantepec, where the Government, in its strenuous efforts to save the situation in the North, has visibly weakened its effectiveness and given an opportunity for a revival of the revolutionary movement under Zapata and various other rebel chiefs. At this moment the State of Sinaloa, with the exception of a few coast towns, and the entire State of Guerrero, with the exception of Acapulco, which is in danger, are in revolt against the Government. In the States of Morelos, Puebla and Tlaxcala authority is divided between the revolutionists and the Government. In the States of Tamaulipas, Veracruz and Chiapas and in the Isthmian part of the State of Oaxaca there are intermittent and dangerous outbreaks, the existence of large bands of brigands and a general insecurity of life and property. The States of Tabasco, Campeche and Yucatan remain, so far as I am able to ascertain, comparatively quiet.

It must not be understood that the Government gains no victories or that the tendency of public opinion is always pessimistic. On the contrary, in the majority of cases where encounters occur I believe the Government forces are victorious, and in the midst of the general depression and gloom there are days when it appears to be regaining its lost prestige and when public opinion inclines to the view that it may finally emerge out of its difficulties. Something more than a week ago the energetic action of the Government in sending military relief to Torreon and Durango coupled with the demonstrations of support and adhesion from all political parties in this and other cities aroused hopes that the nation might be united for its salvation. But these hopes have been largely if not wholly dissipated by the violent and hostile opposition of the lower classes to public demonstrations by the wealthy and aristocratic class who wished to testify adhesion to the Government, by the stupid and ill-timed attacks on de la Barra by the friends of Madero and by their published and open warnings and threats against him in the event that he carries out his announced intention of returning to take up his residence in Mexico. These elements, which might have afforded timely support to the Madero administration, have again been driven into opposition and in public meetings and in the press are indulging in unstinted criticism of the weakness and impotency of the Government and of the crudeness and narrowness of Madero's closest supporters. Thus while there has been no marked change in the material situation during the last week, the violence of political discussion, the lack of a conciliatory policy on the part of the Government and its unlawful practices in the matter of impressment in the army and with reference to the press have brought about in an intensified way the general pessimism which with the exception of this brief interval has existed during the last three months.

The unrest and apprehension in this city, which subsided considerably during the last week, are again markedly apparent. The general situation has something to do with this and the economic situation, which is daily becoming increasingly acute, has more, but the supposed unprotected state of the city, the proximity of rebel bands to the South and armed encounters almost at the gates of the city are in my opinion the real disturbing causes. The emigration of all classes of foreigners, including Americans, continues but I have no means of estimating its volume or the possibility of its continuance or discontinuance. Americans, believing that they had nothing to fear here except mob violence, have, since the perfection of their organization for the defense of their homes and property, been inclined to look more cheerfully on the situation. According to the reports made to me they will in case of necessity be able to concentrate within a fairly short time a well armed and equipped body of twelve hundred men. The Germans are also well organized and have succeeded in securing two machine guns. The excitement and activity seems to be greater in the German colony than in any other in Mexico. This is, I believe, largely due to the deep impression created by the Covadonga outrage and the Torreon massacre. The Spanish, French and English colonies are also organized and armed. I have carefully advised our nationals to avoid everything which could possibly give offense to Mexican public opinion, to indicate clearly that they wish simply to be aids to the officers of the law in the protection of property and their own homes and that under no circumstances must they allow themselves to be drawn aside from the clearly defined purpose of their organization. I anticipate no difficulties on this score.

The President's proclamation of March 2, 1912, and the notice to Americans by this Embassy, which was issued in conformity therewith, at first produced considerable excitement and some misinterpretation, which I believe was due almost entirely to the deeply rooted belief which has been in the mind of everyone that whenever intervention had been determined upon it would be heralded by a Presidential proclamation. After a few days, however, the real intent and true meaning of the proclamation was understood and its reassuring effect on Americans and its sobering one on Mexicans cannot be doubted or questioned. The President's proclamation of March 14, 1912, had a most excellent effect in official and diplomatic circles, where our alleged contribution to the strength of the rebellion has been a matter of frequent and severe criticism. But I have yet to note a single expression of appreciation from the press or from any prominent man in unofficial life. This singular lack of comprehension of our benevolent and patient attitude under most trying circumstances towards the Mexican Republic and the almost national tendency to forget great and substantial benefits conferred and to loudly call attention to trivial offenses is a psychological condition which it is wise to understand and to always anticipate and in our dealings with Mexico it will be well to be satisfied with the knowledge that our actions will stand the test of impartial history and may not be impeached in the wider domain of Latin-American public opinion.

                              I am, my dear Mr. Knox,
                              Very sincerely yours,
                              (signed) Henry Lane Wilson

T E L E G R A M   R E C E I V E D

                              FROM: Mexico City

                              DATED: April 12, 1912

                              REC'D: 6:22 a.m.

Secretary of State,
    Washington.

    April 12, 9 p.m.

    Consul at Aguascalientes reports holding up, by Revolutionists, of
train from Guanajuato to Silao and that American conductor (name not
given) was fatally shot; all passengers and employees maltreated. Also
reports wrecking of train at Irapuato and killing of American engineer,
Zachariah Farmer.

    The representatives of American railway servants on Mexican
National Railways advised me today that such servants would go out in
a body on April seventeenth. In view of the lack of candor which the
Government and the President have shown in this affair, and their
failure to keep distinct promises, I believe efforts to save the situation
will be unavailing. The representatives of American Railway servants
have expressed to me their deep appreciation of the sympathetic
attitude of this Embassy and of the Washington Government. The whole
affair reflects little credit on the Mexican Government and is bound to
reveal many pathetic aspects.

    American colony here has not yet received its ammunition but it
will probably arrive tomorrow or Sunday.

    The killing of Manager Walth of the Esmeralda Plantation, in the
State of Vera Cruz, seems to have been accompanied by circumstances

of incredible barbarity. I have instructed Consuls at Vera Cruz and Salina Cruz to investigate and report.

I have no official report relative to the killing of Fountain at Parral and will act solely on Department's instructions.

WILSON

T E L E G R A M   R E C E I V E D

FROM: Mexico City,
          Mexico

DATED: April 13, 1912

REC'D: April 14, 1912
          10:45 a.m.

Secretary of State,
     Washington.

     April 13, 8 p.m.

Without definite details it is apparent that the situation in the States of Sinaloa, Michoacan Guerrero, Morelos, Chiapas, Veracruz and Puebla is growing worse. This opinion is based largely upon unofficial reports to the Embassy which constitute practically its only source of information at this time.

In this city the financial operations of the Madero family are causing much alarm and criticism. Mr. Brown, President of the National Railways and a Director of the Banco National, informed me today that it was generally believed in financial circles that the Madero family had sent out of the country five million gold in the last month and that this was producing a visible perturbation in the financial situation. If the information which reaches the Department conforms with that received by this Embassy from official private sources, I think it advisable that the President should begin to consider the possibility of having in certain eventualities to send troops into the State of Chihuahua and Guerrero to protect American interests and lives against the bandits under the command of Orozco which seems to be bitterly anti-American in policy and utterly disregardful of international obligations. I believe this question should have the serious consideration of the President, it always being understood that any such action would be directed against rebels and that the National authority would be respected wherever found in existence. If the Department agrees with me (?) (?) in the expediency of this measure I think I should be instructed to sound the Mexican Government as to its attitude.

WILSON

T E L E G R A M   R E C E I V E D

FROM: Mexico City

DATED: April 24, 1912

REC'D: April 25, 1912
1:07 a.m.

Secretary of State,
Washington.

April 24, 8 p.m.

The city of Cuernavaca seems to be completely beleaguered by Rebels to the number of four thousand (estimated) and the probabilities are that it will be surrendered before long. The situation thus produced will be that the Rebels holding practical control of the States of Morelos, Guerrero and a part of Puebla will be in a position to move in strong and increasing numbers toward Mexico City. Should the Federals suffer defeat in the north which seems probable the resulting situation for this city will become serious.

The tone of the local press continues to be malignant and provocative and the Government which suppressed an American paper for publishing the news though giving the Government editorial support makes no effort to modify such utterances.

It is reported on the streets that a motion will be made in the Chamber of Deputies to disarm Americans in this city.

I am holding Department's April 24, 11 a.m. until tomorrow in the hope that a better disposition may be shown by the Government.

                              WILSON

(Department's April 24, 11 a.m. - Importation of arms ammunition for Americans at Tampico, etc.).

T E L E G R A M   R E C E I V E D

FROM: Mexico City

DATED: April 26, 1912

REC'D: April 27, 1912
         5:30 A.M.

Secretary of State,
    Washington, D. C.

    April 26, 9 P.M.

    CONFIDENTIAL. Mr. Oscar Branif, one of the wealthiest men in Mexico, of American origin but Mexican nationality, called upon me today and confidentially informed me that Orozco was receiving the financial aid and support of an organization of many of the wealthiest men in Mexico and that his triumph would lead to the control of affairs by the best elements in Mexico who would restore the prestige of the Government and enter into intimate and cordial relations with our Government. He said that the conviction of this organization was that the Madero Government was doomed and that its present policy was to take precautions against anarchical conditions which might follow and that he was satisfied that these precautions would be effective. Among other names in the organization he mentioned de la Barra. The Department will recall Branif as the representative of Diaz at the conference between that Government and Madero during the Madero Revolution. Mr. Branif stated that his purpose in advising me frankly of the situation was that the Department might understand that chaos would not follow the fall of the Madero Government. I listened attentively to Mr. Branif's statement but made no comment whatever.

                                        WILSON

FINCA CHICAGO

April 28th, 1913

Mr. Jacob Mansar
    Altadena,
        California.

Dear Mr. Mansar:

Since writing you last on March 29th, there has been a continual string of trouble. This trouble has not interfered much with the work, but it has completely stopped my correspondence and the time that I otherwise would have put in on office work and correspondence, has been taken up with bandit troubles.

On Tuesday, March 25th, 170 soldiers of the 31st batallion revolted in San Juan Bautista. They attacked the Banks and big business houses, did a lot of looting, took quite a lot of money and valuable merchandise, and terrorized the town generally. They then took possession of the River Steam Boat, MACUSPANA, intending to go to Cardenas and Huimanguillo, and from the latter place they were to have come on up this way into Chiapas, but in attempting to go through the Pigua canal, the Macuspana turned turtle with them. Of the original 170 soldiers, 138 were drowned, 10 were caught and shot, leaving 22 to be accounted for. Later reports state that several more of the 22 have been caught and shot.

Sunday, April 6th, some bandits took Huimanguillo. They shot Colonel Martinez, the Jefe Politico, and 5 others, in fact they shot all of the officials that did not skip. They robbed the merchants and all others, burned documents from some of the offices, burned the furniture and the houses of their enemies and held the town for 6 days or until the federal forces arrived from San Juan, then the bandits moved up to the Paso de Chiocacan, about 2 leagues from here and there they remained until routed out by a small federal force on the morning of April 17th. At this fight 4 of the bandits were killed and a number of saddle horses taken by the federals. The report comes today that there are still quite a large number of these bandits camped in the woods near the Paso de Chicoacan. We frequently hear shots and see armed men passing along the road, but so far they have not attacked the place; they have attacked other fincas and have been very brutal.

On Wednesday, April 9th, I had the house fortified. To do this I used the large steel plates which Adolph purchased to make rubber washing tanks. These plates I backed up with sacks, boxes, steel drum barrels and cans filled with sand. The windows are all barricaded with sacks of sand, the corridor likewise and the doors all re-enforced from the inside with timbers. We eat, sleep and go out to the works with our rifles at hand and one man is always on guard. Naturally there is only one thing to do if they come and that is to fight, for they show no consideration to those who surrender to them.

Thursday, April 17th, 13 federal soldiers arrived here, they were very rough but went away without doing any damage. They however pocketed some of my toilet articles and took some money away from some of the workmen. These were also men from the 31st batallion. On Thursday, April 24th, 50 soldiers of the 31st arrived here about 4 p.m. and remained all night. This time the Lieutenant was with them and they behaved very well. They left here on Friday morning.

While here the Colonel of the 31st reported that the Steamer Mezcalapa had been attacked on her way up from San Juan, and that all of the mail had been taken. There are reports of other attacks on the mails. So far we have had only one mail since this trouble began and that was a very small one, which was sent by a boatman who slipped up in the night. On Wednesday, the 16th, I sent a man into town, and I hear that he is still in the town, afraid to come out. The roads are not at all safe and only the bandits are traveling. We are running low on provisions and some time this week I must go to town and by some means send out a supply. Arrangements had been made to have a lot of provisions for the men delivered here but this trouble makes them all afraid, and now I must go at it in some other way. In the mean time we are not getting any papers, consequently we do not know what is going on in other parts of the country.

With this small mail that arrived was a message from Manuel Alonso saying that he would be in San Juan the 20th and here at the finca the 24th or the 25th, but it is now the 28th and there is no telling what may have happened to him.

The gates leading into the finca are all chained and locked. The bandits were here at the lower gates one afternoon, but for some reason they did not come in. Another report has just this minute arrived, saying that there are 40 bandits camped at Chicoacan. Well this gets on ones nerves a little, I hope that it will soon end.

I do not know when I can send this letter and it may be that I will make some additions to same before I get a chance to mail it.

Monday, May 5th, 1913.

Since writing the above, the chances of being attacked seemed so serious that I have devoted all of my time to keeping a lookout and keeping everything in a constant state of preparedness. I have kept an all night guard, here inside of the house, composed of Powell, Fry, Jesus, (the bookkeeper) and myself. In fact the bandits have passed here in large and small numbers, both by day and by night, I have frequently watched them from the house, with the aid of a pair of field glasses. They frequently stopped at the gate, but as that was kept locked, they would have to cut the wire to get in, but in all cases, so far, they have gone on without molesting us, though they have robbed and commited depredations on nearby plantations.

The report now comes that they have gone off to the llanos near the river Pedrigal and that their leaders have skipped out with all the cash results of the various robberies. Since writing you on the 28th, the bandits, or Zapatistas, as they call themselves, attacked

Huimanguillo again, but were driven off with a loss of 4 killed and some wounded. It is now claimed that they have split up into small gangs, but that does not help the situation so far as we are concerned.

There is a man who has agreed to go into town with a canoe to bring out some very much needed provisions and I am sending this along in the hopes that it will reach you.

So far I hear nothing further from Manuel Alonso and the canoe loaded with my personal effects and some supplies for the place.

Yours truly,
(signed) G. B. Mann

Copy to Davis and Gavito.

AMERICAN CONSULATE
San Luis Potosi, Mexico

No. 59   April 30, 1912

SUBJECT: Political Conditions in San Luis Potosi.

The Honorable
    The Secretary of State,
        Washington.

Sir:

I have the honor to report that brigandage is increasing in this district, especially on the extreme boundaries of the district to the south, the east and the northeast, and that insecurity is somewhat more general than formerly reported.

Americans telegraph this office that a band of twenty robbers has appeared very near to the American colony of San Dieguito, some one hundred and ten miles east of this city, that they have threatened the property of Americans and have threatened to kill Mr. L. M. McCrocklin and family and to burn his property. It is also reported that at least one young American (Lauder) has been captured by the authorities with bandits in that locality yesterday. At my request the Governor of the State has telegraphed orders for thirty rurales to go immediately to Micos to protect Mr. McCrocklin and others.

A group of nearly two hundred rebels are operating very near to the plantation of Vice Consul Dickinson, in the district of Abasolo, Guanajuato, near Salamanca, and they completely routed the Federal force sent against them last week.

Another group has been operating in the vicinity of Tula, Tamaulipas, about ninety-five miles northeast of this city, while a small band infests the mountains surrounding the town of Rio Verde, some sixty miles easterly from this city.

The Governor states that brigandage is increasing, in spite of his efforts, especially in the eastern part of the State, which consists of dense jungles covering broken country, with no roads, rendering pursuit almost impossible. There are in that locality more than fifty thousand native Indians who do not speak the Spanish language and who have never been subjected to Government; they are, however, loyal to the Government at the present time.

Approximately one hundred and ten American railway employees, with their families, have left this district and returned to the United States. There are left in this city about seventy men at present, and in the district outside this city about the same number. The American residents in this district have been reduced from some fifteen hundred to less than six hundred in all.

The Cinco Estrellas Mining Company, of Pinos, Zacatecas, some forty miles west of this city, has closed down, throwing more than three hundred and fifty men out of employment. This is an American Company.

Some volunteers raised in this district have been sent to Torreon. Laborers going through on trains have been taken and pressed into the ranks here. The remnants of the 7th and 13th Regiments which occupied this garrison have been sent to Torreon, and a part of the 10th Regiment is now here, not more than two hundred men. The protection is insufficient.

Many native families from plantations and from smaller towns have taken refuge in the city of San Luis Potosi.

The State of San Luis Potosi has again been obliged to borrow money for current expenses, giving public real estate as security.

The anti-American feeling has increased. The local papers almost daily have published items and articles criticizing or insulting Americans or their Government. While these articles have appeared in the Catholic paper, they have also appeared in other small newspapers. Americans have in some cases been personally threatened. The articles referred to in the local newspapers are considered too foolish to quote or discuss.

It is believed hopeless for foreigners to attempt to secure the good will of these people by means of justice or generosity. They do not understand the motives or spirit of our Government or our people. It is believed that in this district the people have demonstrated their incapacity for representative government. It is believed further that disintegration has set in and that unless checked by force all that has been accomplished in the way of civilization and civil order will be lost. The lower class of the people would naturally prefer a crude communism; the wealthier class would prefer the form of a landed aristocracy; with both these tendencies the foreign interests and the foreign influence come in direct conflict. The class feeling is so much stronger than national feeling that no system will be successful which does not recognize their social differences and democracy is therefore (and for other reasons) impracticable. Even to the wealthier classes a chaos in which they can maintain their distinctions is preferable to real democracy. These people fear humiliation more than they fear financial loss or loss of nationality.

Due diligence is not used in prosecuting or in punishing sedition. Disloyalty is prevalent; seditious plots are suspected. Robbery and disloyalty meet slight punishment or none at all; news is suppressed or distorted. There is no cohesion even for purposes of defence. In such a situation it is impossible to predict. If a crisis should come as the result of gradual demoralization it is feared that no one may be able to foresee the exact time when danger to Americans may become actual and immediate.

I have the honor to be, Sir,

Your obedient servant,
(signed) Wilbert L. Bonney
Consul.

AMERICAN CONSULAR SERVICE
Oaxaca, Mexico

C.G. No. 61.   May 2nd, 1912

Hon. Arnold Shanklin,
        American Consul General,
            Mexico, D. F.

Sir:

Governor Montiel, in a public speech a few days since, stated that his first aim, during his term of office, would be to at all times, afford to foreigners resident in Oaxaca, all necessary guarantees and protection.

An outbreak on the part of natives in the valley some 15 miles south of Oaxaca, has resulted in some thirty dead, besides wounded. The trouble seems to be on account of the natives not getting land, which under the Madero administration, they were promised. The outbreak is directed against several large haciendas, but commenced on the hacienda owned by C. A. Hamilton, an American citizen. It is rumored that there are behind the uprising, two state deputies, or members of legislature, who are not content with the present provisional governor.

Other than stated, matters continue in the state, as reported, so far as known.

I am, Sir,

                        Your obedient servant,
                        (signed) E. M. Lawton
                        American Consular Agent

AMERICAN CONSULATE
San Luis Potosi, Mexico

No. 60   May 6, 1912

SUBJECT: Political Conditions in San Luis Potosi.

The Honorable
    The Secretary of State,
        Washington.

Sir:

I have the honor to attach hereto a newspaper clipping containing an alleged interview with Senor Manuel Calero, the new Mexican Ambassador to the United States, purporting to be taken from the New York Times.

The statements credited to Senor Calero regarding the situation in Mexico are in conflict with consular reports from this district, and in so far as concerns this district the views attributed to Senor Calero are essentially untrue, although this State is at present one of the most orderly in Mexico.

1.   Contrary to the statement credited to Senor Calero, American women have been insulted on the streets of this city, not by bandits but by soldiers in uniform with their officers present, by students and by others. American women will not now go on the streets unattended.

2.   The statement that there is no anti-foreign sentiment in Mexico, so far as concerns this district, is untrue in the highest degree. Americans have been insulted, threatened and warned by Mexicans. Offensive newspaper articles directed against Americans and their Government have frequently appeared, at times containing improper and malicious suggestions. Public speakers on the streets, and priests in their churches have expressed strong animosity toward foreigners. In short, instances of anti-foreign feeling are of daily occurrence.

3.   The statement that Americans are the only foreigners who have left Mexico is also untrue. In this district Spaniards and Germans have suffered and have been more alarmed than Americans, and many have left the country. Citizens of Great Britain, Persia and Turkey have appealed to this office for advice, and in four cases they have expressed a desire to become American citizens. Many of the better class Mexican families have gone to the United States, and many others have left their plantations, and the small towns and taken refuge in this city.

4.   The statement credited to Senor Calero that Americans have left Mexico because of exaggerated press reports is highly incorrect so far as concerns this district. The press has been almost silent regarding San Luis Potosi. Americans here have not taken their impressions from the newspapers. Many of our resident Americans have lived here for twenty years and upward. Their alarm has been caused by local conditions alone, by threats, by lack of public protection, and

by the attitude of the lower and middle classes. These Americans have for the most part sent their families to the United States; they have armed themselves and are prepared to abandon their homes and business in an emergency, or to defend themselves if abandonment is not possible. These men do not act hastily nor without cause.

5.   The statement attributed to Senor Calero to the effect that Americans quit Mexico because of a misinterpretation of a proclamation by President Taft is not true of this district.

6.   The statement attributed to Senor Calero that outside of four States the people are contented and happy does not represent the conditions in San Luis Potosi.

I have the honor to be, Sir,

Your obedient servant,
(signed) Wilbert L. Bonney
Consul

Enclosure: Newspaper clipping.

TIIE NEW YORK TIMES

The only foreigners in Mexico who are at all uneasy and who are leaving that country as a result of "exaggerated press reports of conditions in that country" are Americans, said Senor Manuel Calero, the new Mexican Ambassador to the United States, last night.

Senor Calero arrived here yesterday on the Ward liner Mexico from Veracruz, and may go to Washington today. Whether or not he goes to the capital will depend on the nature of the information he will get by long-distance telephone from the Mexican Charge d'Affaires today and by telegraph from the City of Mexico.

The new Ambassador is young for his post - not much more than forty years old. He speaks English fluently. He is stopping at the Hotel Astor and it was there that he received newspaper men last night to whom he talked at length with somewhat startling frankness of conditions in his more or less troubled country. In the first place he said that Francisco Madero was fulfilling the promises he made when he started the revolution that overthrew Diaz.

Then he declared that there was no revolution in Mexico, and that only four States were affected by the present unrest, and only one of those four -- Chihuahua -- seriously; that reports of the Japanese getting a foothold in the Gulf of California were ridiculous; that few people in America knew anything at all about Mexico, and that when President Taft issued his warning to Americans to leave Mexico many Americans resident in Mexico thought they could "read between the lines," and lost no time in quitting the country.

Senor Calero is extremely courteous and is a representative of the highest type of Mexican. He has been in public life many years and has held important positions in the administrations of Diaz, de la Barra, and Madero, being a member of the Cabinets of both de la Barra and Madero. Under Diaz he was an Assistant Secretary of Agriculture.

"Now, gentlemen," said the Ambassador when he received the reporters, "I am at your service, and will try to answer any question that is proper which you may desire to ask me."

"Well, suppose you tell us what the real conditions in Mexico are?" was the first question.

TELLS OF CHAT WITH ROOSEVELT.

"Well," the Ambassador replied, "I will begin with a reference to my visit to Chicago four years ago, when I went as a sightseer, so to speak, to witness the deliberations of the Republican National Convention. Senator (then Minister of Foreign Affairs) Elihu Root was there, and after the convention adjourned he asked me to visit Washington and be presented to President Roosevelt. We learned, however, that President Roosevelt, had left Washington and had gone to Oyster Bay, and so I went there to see him and he invited me to luncheon.

"In the course of a conversation, the President made a remark which was very true. He said that the people in America knew very little about their neighbors to the South, meaning the Latin Americans. He said that we Latin Americans were a puzzle to you Americans, and that is a fact. If the rest of the people in the United States had the knowledge of Mexico that Mr. Roosevelt has, it would be well for all concerned, for a great majority of the people in the United States know nothing whatever about our country.

"Now, take the alleged troubles that beset Mexico at the present time, which have been so grossly exaggerated and which, as a matter of fact, are confined to four States -- a very small part of our country when you stop to think. All of the rest of the country is at peace and the people are contented and happy. In the four States most of the trouble is caused by a few bandits whose subjection is only a matter of time.

"For instance, I have recently received a letter from Dr. Albert Oxner, one of the most distinguished surgeons in Chicago. Dr. Oxner some time ago bought a ranch in Colima, one of the Pacific Coast States. It was more for sport than anything else that Dr. Oxner acquired the ranch. Recently he was in Mexico, and on his way to Colima he came to the City of Mexico and then traveled across the country to his ranch.

"When he returned to Chicago he wrote me a letter in which he said that he was surprised on his trip across the country to find the people so happy and satisfied generally. Nowhere did he hear any talk about revolutions. That is the report of an unbiased visitor, which is much better than that of an American railroad conductor who has been discharged and who gives out stories about alarming conditions in Mexico.

RIDICULES EXAGGERATED REPORTS.

"Again, I remember that a few days ago when I was in Havana there was a story, an Associated Press story from Mexico, which stated that American women were being insulted in Mexico, and that American men were being beheaded. That story was not only false, but very stupid. In some particular isolated case it is possible that a bandit may have insulted a woman, but is that a reason to say that American women are not safe in Mexico? Assuredly not.

"If a white woman in one of your Southern States is insulted by a negro, is that a reason to say that women are not safe in this country, or if a train is held up in some part of this country, is that ground for sending out a report that your country is in a state of anarchy?

"Again, I would remind you that it is a very curious phenomenon that we have in Mexico so many people who are not Mexicans. Remember that is Mexico there are a great many nationalities represented. There are Germans, English, Americans, French, Norwegians, in fact practically all of the nations are represented in Mexico, yet the fact remains that the only foreigners in Mexico who have left the country are the Americans. There was no reason for their leaving. They got out because of exaggerated press reports, while the other foreigners, the British, the French, the Germans, etc., stayed and attended quietly to their business affairs and have not had any trouble.

"There is no anti-foreign sentiment in Mexico and it is deplorable that Americans have listened to these exaggerated reports and in many instances left their business and quit Mexico. When President Taft issued his perfectly well-meaning message in which he advised Americans to leave, many of your countrymen in Mexico thought they could read between the lines and see something more serious than what the President really said.

"Of course Mr. Taft had no idea of giving a double meaning to his message, but there were those who had an idea such a meaning was there and they were among those who quit the country.

"Of course some American interests have suffered. They suffered considerably during your own civil war, did they not? They must have suffered considerably as a result of Sherman's march to the sea.

"We are not in that condition in Mexico, for we have no civil war, despite the fact that there are some bandits operating in four States, one of them -- Morelos -- the smallest except one of all the Mexican States. In those States the bandits have destroyed some property, but that is not civil war any more than a train robbery or a holdup in some section of the United States would constitute such a condition."

"What about the United States army transport Buford going to the west coast of Mexico to rescue Americans? Do you think that voyage is justified?" Senor Calero was asked.

"I have not received reports as to conditions in Sinaloa, the State in which the Americans referred to are," the Ambassador replied, "but I understand that there is some unrest in a part of that State."

"How about the Japanese and the fishing concessions to them in Magdalena Bay?" was another question.

"There is not a Japanese question in Mexico," Senor Calero replied, "and this talk about the Japanese and Magdalena Bay is ridiculous. It is absurd that you Americans should be exercised [sic] about the granting of a private fishing concession to Japanese. Such concessions are held by the English, by Norwegians, and by Mexicans, and it is nothing more nor less than a business transaction, in which the concessionaries are responsible to the Mexican government, and to no other government in the world.

"The whole thing, as some have tried to make it look, is absolutely untrue.

LODGE ALL WRONG, HE SAYS.

"Before I left Mexico City I saw that Senator Lodge had asked for a Senatorial inquiry into the alleged Japanese situation as regards Magdalena Bay. I made a report, for I was then Minister of Foreign Affairs, in Mr. Madero's cabinet, in which I stated that there was no truth in the report that the concession had anything to do with the Japanese government. Senator Lodge, for whom I have the greatest respect, was entirely wrong. Of course, if they want to investigate let them do it, but it will be time wasted, because they will be investigating something that does not exist.

"The truth of the whole matter is that a few years ago a concession for fishing privileges was granted to a private Japanese enterprise. There is nothing extraordinary about that, for the same thing is true of citizens of many other nations. All the concessions are the same."

"What about the report that the Japanese government is backing this private enterprise of its citizens, and that among those who have been looking over the promises mentioned in the concession is a member of the Japanese parliament?" Senor Calero was asked.

"I don't know anything about any such member of the Japanese parliament. For all you know, your Japanese cook may be a powerful man in Japan. Our dealings are with the concessionaries and not the Japanese government. For that matter, there are a great many Japanese in Hawaii, and many of them, I am told, are veterans of the Russo-Japanese War," Senor Calero said.

The Ambassador brought his interview to a close with a reference to the conditions in the great border State of Chihuahua, the largest of all the Mexican States.

"As regards conditions in Chihuahua," Senor Calero said, "I read today that Orozco says he hopes the country will follow the Liberal party, indicating that he considers himself the leader of the Liberal movement. That is absurd. What he should have said was the Anti-Liberal Party.

****

AMERICAN CONSULAR SERVICE
Oaxaca, Mexico

C. G. No. 62.   May 6th, 1912

Hon. Arnold Shanklin,
        American Consul General,
            Mexico, D. F.

Sir:

Reporting on the political situation, I have to state that in the valley south of this city, for the past five days, the Indians, who have been made to believe to some extent, that Governor Juarez was poisoned, have risen, and though not well organized, and but poorly armed, have attacked and sacked several haciendas and small ranches. Only one American hacienda has been attacked, which was reported in my last bi-weekly report, and there the soldiers repelled the bandits. No attempt is made to follow up the advantage, on part of the soldiers, as they are largely in the minority, though probably the superior force, on account of arms and organization. There are about 600 in the combined guerrilla forces. The soldiers and rurales number less than one hundred. Two of the state deputies, Olivera and Colmenares are believed to be behind the movement. The Indians hurrah also, for General (?) Olivera. This is the Olivera who has issued such inflamatory proclamations against Americans.

The American colony here is now organizing and stocking the American Club building, with provisions and arms, to be a rendevouz, in case of necessity. Probably premature, but also to a certain extent prudent. In case of anarchistic conditions arising, which is hardly expected, the colony will be able to hold off a very superior number.

The attempt of citizens, some weeks back, to organize a paid civic guard, has come to naught. Matters other than reported, remain much as previously stated.

I am, Sir,

> Your obedient servant,
> (signed) E. M. Lawton
> American Consular Agent

AMERICAN CONSULATE
Frontera, Tab., Mexico

No. 202   May 28, 1912

SUBJECT: Peaceful conditions prevailing in Tabasco.
                    Predicament in which Americans would find themselves
                    should a rigid quarantine be enforced in the United
                    States against this port on account of yellow fever
                    epidemic.

The Honorable
    The Secretary of State,
        Washington.

Sir:

I have the honor to inform the Department that absolute order
prevails in all sections of this state, and as reported in the telegram
from this office of the 25th instant, a confirmation copy of which is
herewith enclosed, no revolutionists or revolutionary movement exists in
Tabasco. The entire state is remarkably peaceful and will no doubt
remain so as long as the federal forces are not withdrawn. The entire
force of federals with the exception of 20 or 25 which are detached from
the main body from time to time for service at points where there is the
least indication of local disturbances, are stationed in the capital San
Juan Bautista.

Col. Juan A. Poloney has 200 federals of the 31st battalion under
his command and Capt. Alfonso Blea 100 federals of the 19th battalion;
this force could be increased by a reserve body of 75 to 100 state
rurales which the state government can equip whenever it should be
necessary to place them in the field for active service; these forces will
in the near future be increased by the 100 recruits referred to in my
despatch No. 200 of May 18, 1912, and telegram of the 25th instant.
"Gegmy", as soon as they are properly drilled and accoutred they will

be formed into a corps of federal rurales providing they can be trusted; if not they will be incorporated into the 31st battalion.

These recruits arrived in a deplorable condition; many were in a semi-naked state, others had been brutally punished and all were extremely filthy; as stated in my telegram of above date they will be a grave menace to San Juan Bautista, and may aggravate the outbreak of yellow fever in that city, becoming themselves victims to this disease unless the most rigid sanitary measure are adopted to improve their wretched condition.

Quite recently the managers of several of the American rubber plantations in this state and northern Chiapas have displayed a tendency to leave the plantations in their charge to the care of native managers and take up their residence in this port so as to be ready to leave for the United States by the fruit steamers plying between this port and Galveston, Texas, every week or ten days; the fleet consists of the Swedish steamer Disa, 804 tons, Captain: P. Ingvarsson; steamer Burstad, Norwegian, 960 tons, Captain: H. M. Ellingsen, and the Fagertun, 851 tons, also Norwegian Captain: Magnus Mathisen; these steamers have accommodations for 10 to 17 passengers, trip from this port to Galveston about 70 hours, passage $25.00 gold.

At present F. McAllister, manager of the Utah Mexican Rubber Co. of Salt Lake City, Utah, with his wife and his assistant, F. B. Parkinson, who is also accompanied by his wife, have left the above plantation in charge of a native manager; they will remain here until order has been fully restored in Mexico or they may depart at a moment's notice for the United States in case they should consider it imprudent to return to the plantation.

This consulate has been informed that the managers of other American rubber plantations in this state may also adopt this course in case the political situation in this country does not improve in the near future.

Should the present outbreak of yellow fever in San Juan Bautista cause a strict quarantine to be enforced in the United States against this port, Americans would find themselves in a serious predicament, in case the political situation should assume a threatening aspect and compel them to depart for the United States. I have refrained from mentioning this matter to Americans but deem it my duty to call the Department's attention to this matter and beg to be informed whether Americans from this state would under proper restrictions be allowed to land in the United States should it become absolutely necessary for them to leave Tabasco.

I beg to enclose copy of a letter received from Dr. J. F. Eaves who is the Special Quarantine Inspector for the state of Texas in this port.

I have the honor to be, Sir,
Your Obedient servant,
(signed) A. J. Lespinarse
American Consul

[Editor's note: Enclosure mentioned in above text not included here.]

AMERICAN CONSULATE
Mazatlan, Mexico

No. 224   June 13th, 1912

SUBJECT: Political Situation.

The Honorable
    The Secretary of State,
        Washington.

Sir:

I have the honor to report on the situation. On June 9th, General Delgado with two hundred men and artillery left for the capital, Culiacan. On arrival he, it is said, took over the governorship, also appointed Col. Gotari, Prefect of Mazatlan, thus putting the state under military rule. General Ojeda, who had left the previous week on an expedition, it is claimed, had several skirmishes and killed a few of the rebels, and hung half a dozen. He issued orders for Panuco and Copala to be abandoned within eight days, as he considered them to be nests of bandits. The former has large Spanish mining interests; the latter some American interests. All the inhabitants of these places are leaving.

In the northern part of the state conditions are improving. In the southern part it seems to be growing worse. The entire country between here and Tepic is filled with roaming bands of bandits. When the Federal forces approach, they flee; later on they return and resume their occupation of robbing and looting.

If guard is not sent to Quimiches at once, it will be useless as it will be too late to plant crops, and I have so wired the Embassy. A guard of 30 soldiers has been sent to Concha to protect American interests there. If they remain, while they are there, order will be maintained; but once they leave, conditions will be worse; as revenge will be sought and the houses of the American Company will without doubt be burnt.

I have the honor to be, Sir,

Your obedient servant,
(signed) Wm. E. Alger
American Consul

AMERICAN CONSULATE

Tampico, Mexico

No. 577   July 3, 1912

SUBJECT: Copies of Campaign Literature distributed
              in the State of Veracruz.

The Honorable

   The Secretary of State,

      Washington, D. C.

Sir:

I have the honor to enclose herewith some copies of campaign literature which were distributed recently in the State of Veracruz. This literature is evidently being distributed by those who are opposing Mr. Braniff in campaign for the Governorship of the State of Veracruz.

I have the honor to be, Sir,

Your obedient servant,

(signed) Clarence Arkell

American Consul

Enclosures: As stated.

Enclosure of despatch No. 577. Tampico, Mexico,
July 3, 1912.

M I S T E R   T H O M A S   B R A N I F F

A M E R I C A N O,

CANDIDATO AL GOBIERNO DE VERACRUZ.
****
Tomamos de "El Grito del Pueblo" lo siguiente:

VERACRUZANOS:

No olvideis quesel 30 del presente se celebrara

en la ciudad de Cordoba la

GRAN COMBINACION

para sacar avante la candiatura

MALPICA - BRANIFF

And Justice? Solo cuando me quiera,
and nadie chille pues me se emperra!
Del MONEY, solo yo dare cuenta,
Conmigo, BRANIFF! nadie se enfrenta.

Mi ser el yandee now designado
for ser GOBERNADOR of this Estado
Mi ha dado Lagos mucho dinero,
Y AQUI ME IMPONE, Mister Madero.

ZEKE.
****

If you cannot translate this composition into pure Spanish,

just come down and look for me in Morelos.
****

Enclosure to Despatch No. 577, Tampico, Mexico,
July 3, 1912.

M I S T E R   T H O M A S   B R A N I F F

A M E R I C A N O,

CANDIDATO AL GOVIERNO DE VERACRUZ.

****

Tomamos de "El Grito del Pueblo" lo siguiente:

Mi ser el yandee now designado
for ser GOBERNADOR of this Estado,
Mi ha dado Lagos mucho dinero,
Y AQUI ME IMPONE Mister Madero.

Mi ser hermano del VOLUNTARIO,
TORERO, AVIATOR and HONORARIO,
or Albert Braniff el Gran Soldado
hecho al chaleco por "OJO PARADO".

Yo quiere a Uds. VERACRUZANOS,
(porque son todos my dear paisanos) (?)
darles instruction, civizarlos,
y en aereoplanos contramatarlos.

Dentro de pocotu! 'PUEBLO! vuelas!
and I will give you lots of escuelas
para que aprendas que no hay semilla
que no digiera.......Manuel Bonilla.

And Justice? Solo cuando me quiera,
and nadie chille pues me se emperra!
Del MONEY, solo yo dare cuenta,
Conmigo, BRANIFF! nadie se enfrenta.

Mi ser el yankee now designado
for ser GOVERNADOR of this Estado
Mi ha dado Lagos mucho dinero,
Y AQUI ME IMPONE Mister Madero.

ZEKE.

****

If you cannot translate this composition into pure Spanish,
just come down and look for me in Morelos.

****

Enclosure to Despatch No. 577, Tampico, Mexico,
July 3, 1912.

MR. BRANIFF
A LA PUERTA
****

Ya quedo resuelto, en perjuicio del Estado y para doloroso desengano del pueblo, que el millonario don Thomas Braniff, veracruzano por pura.....casualidad, lance su antipatica e impolitica candidatura al Gobierno de Veracruz, con pasmo de la democracia y estupefaccion del sentido comun. Se nos ha dicho que llego un furgon, cargado con materiales de propaganda, a esta ciudad; que por lo pronto, ya desembolso treinta mil pesos el flamante candidato, y que desembolsara otros tantos mas, si es necesario, para asegurar el triunfo. La candidatura del senor Braniff no tiene ni tendra aceptacion entre los veracruzanos, altivos, pundonorosos, rebeldes a toda humillacion. El senor Braniff jamas podra jactarse, en el remoto case de que triunfe, de poseer el afecto del pueblo, presea que no se vende, que no puede adquirirse no con todos los millones del senor Braniff. El senor Braniff, en caso de que se vea sentado en la silla que ocuparon los Hernandez y Hernandez y los Henriquez, nunca obtendra, como estos, la confianza del pueblo de Veracruz.

Los hombres acaudalados, para quienes todo se alcanza por medio del omnipotente dollar, para quienes honor, poder, talento, virtud, son otras tantas comunes y corrientes mercancias, de facil adquisicion mediante el VIL METAL, estan dando en la locura de figurarse que tambien se compra la conciencia publica. Se engana miserablemente, cuando esa conciencia es la de un pueblo, como el nuestro, disciplinado por la mas gloriosa tradicion, por la mas limpia y envidiable historia.

Don Thomas Braniff, aun cuando trae la llave que franquea todas las puertas, no podra abrir la del corazon del pueblo. Hallara en su CAMPANA politica, muchos aduladores, muchos adeptos a......su bolsillo, muchos admiradores de su caja fuerte; pero simpatizadores de su candidatura, convencidos de que podra labrar la felicidad y la grandeza del Estado, no hallara ni uno entre el millon y medio de veracruzanos.

El primer enemigo que el senor Braniff tiene contra el exito de sus aspiraciones, es la dignidad del pueblo. Este, podra doblegarse ante la fuerza, podra ser sorprendido por la perfidia y el maquiavelismo; pero venderse, a sabiendas, conscientes, como se vende una prostituta, jamas.

Tal vez no triunfe el anhelo popular en los proximos comicios; quizas no sea respetada la voluntad del pueblo.

Quedara vencido, pero no deshonrado; burlado, pero no vendido. Y don Thomas Braniff, sera Gobernador; sera dueno de todo, menos del amor de los altivos y pundonorosos hijos de Veracruz.

Y la historia cuando consigne manana la relacion de sucesos tan escandalosos, sera un juez implacable cuyo fallo pesara con peso de montana soble los conculcadores del derecho y de la justicia.

JALAPA, JUNIO DE 1912.

DE "EL CLARIN".

AMERICAN CONSULAR SERVICE
Oaxaca, Mexico

C. G. No. 90.   August 8th, 1912

Hon. Arnold Shanklin,
     American Consul General,
          Mexico, D. F.

Sir:

I have to report that the campaign which was supposed to have been started against the rebellious district of the Sierra Juarez, was not commenced as I was informed and as I reported. Each day, for many days, the Federal forces have been saying that they would start until now the whole sierras has revolted and local merchants have solicited to the point of insistence, of the Federal government in Mexico, that some action be taken. There are over a thousand troops here, and the local general has been fearful that there was not enough to conduct the campaign and leave a sufficient guard here. Now, it is imperative and today or tomorrow there is to start some 600 men, with arms also to furnish to certain residents of the valley, who are ancient enemies of the serranos. There will be at least 1000 men advance from this side, and there are 450 Federals and 350 loyal serranos, who will assume the offensive who are now isolated in the town of Ixtlan, in the sierras. There are probably at least 5000 rebels to oppose, but how well armed it is not known. Naturally, the matter promises to be serious.

The other parts of the state report also various bands of roving marauders under guise of being rebels. In general, the detachments of rurales and federals are taking very good care of such. The governatorial election results are not yet announced, and there is absolutely no positive assurance to be had as to what the result will be. In the minds of many, this whole affair presents a complication which might produce very serious results. Personally I have no idea that there is any danger affecting more than the disaffected district, and that the other matters will be successfully or satisfactorily settled. In the remote possibility of the routing of the troops to be sent against the serranos, then affairs might take a very serious turn.

A recent issue of the daily paper here known as El Alerta alleges that two Americans have been found to be the ones who are or have been supplying the serranos with arms and ammunition. The paper states that the names are known, but for purpose of further investigation on part of authorities, are withheld for the present. Rumor has it that the men suspicioned are U. R. Burton, who lives at El Parian, this state and who conducts a general store, and another German or German-American named Teufel, living at Nochistlan. I know nothing more than this of the alleged rumors.

It is to be hoped that the Federal Government has really taken some interest in this affair of the Sierra Juarez. It is almost sure that the entire district of the Sierras has revolted, and there are more or less 20,000 fighting men living in said district, and with a reasonably fair complement of arms.

I am, Sir,

Your obedient servant,
(signed) E. M. Lawton
Consular Agent

AMERICAN CONSULATE
Veracruz, Mexico

No. 760.   August 23, 1912

SUBJECT: Report. The Political Situation in General in this
         Consular District.

The Honorable
    The Secretary of State,
        Washington.

Sir:

I have the honor to transmit, herewith enclosed, copies of letters from Americans residing in this consular district, relative to requests for protection, the action taken by the government, and the political conditions in general existing in the districts where they reside and where their properties are located.

From the enclosures it will be noted that these Americans are trying to make the best of circumstances; that they are reasonable in their demands for protection, and that they do not object, in so far as their means will permit, to bearing part of the expenses for the protection asked for.

Although there seems to be a willingness on the part of the government officials to furnish aid and assistance whenever and wherever required, it appears as though there were a lack of system in their movements. Whenever, in response to an urgent call for help, a body of troops is sent, they will either arrive too late; there will not be a sufficient number or they will not remain long enough in the locality to be of any real service. It may be conceded that the number of federal soldiers and rurales available for such service is entirely insufficient, but under proper management, the results obtained with those which are available, would be much more satisfactory.

The garrisons of federals at present maintained in this district, in comparison with those formerly maintained, are greatly reduced. Previously, the garrison in the manufacturing district of Orizaba consisted of a full battalion, at present it is reduced to fifty and sometimes to as low as twenty five men; the same conditions are reported from Jalapa, the state capital. At Veracruz there were two battalions with a total of seven hundred to a thousand men, now there are scarcely a hundred left. This place is now being used as a general drilling station and, frequently, detachments of (so called) volunteers, from twenty-five to one hundred fifty in number, arrive under guard from interior points. These recruits, after receiving some military instruction, are hurried away for active service.

At the present time, bandits are not confining themselves to the stealing of cattle but are assaulting farms and small settlements. Medellin, a village about eight miles from this city, on the Alvarado Ry. was recently visited by a gang of marauders. This gang operated in the neighborhood of Veracruz, moving from one place to another until they had reached a point on the Interoceanic Ry. which lies in an opposite direction from this city to that in which they first operated. Afterward, although they seemed to have disappeared, they were hiding in the woods not ten miles from here. I was told that, when this gang was raiding Medellin, the manager of the Alvarado Ry. had, in response to a call for assistance, a train ready to start at once, but before the officials could decide to send police or federal soldiers, the bandits had had plenty of time to finish their work and depart. Anxiety is still felt for the safety of the city water supply at El Tejar, half a mile from Medellin, and ten policemen have been sent there.

The most recent raid of importance was that on Coatepec, a town of some size in the immediate neighborhood of and connected by a direct Ry. with Jalapa. The object of this band which numbered about eight bandits was to get possession of certain arms and ammunition. After succeeding in this they opened the county prison and liberated about one hundred prisoners. Not until the next day could a train crew be found to take a train with state volunteers to the place. Fighting in the neighboring mountains has been reported between these volunteers and bandits.

Conditions in the mills and factories in the vicinity of Orizaba have been very unsatisfactory ever since the change in the government. Strike after strike at short intervals and nearly always under the most unreasonable pretexts. The managements of the mills have, heretofore, been well disposed to make allowances to settle the petty differences in each instance; this notwithstanding the well known fact that they had very little demand for their product and therefore large stocks of it on hand. In July last, in one of the factories, a laborer was dismissed as an undesirable element. His fellow laborers threatened to lay down their work unless he was reinstated. As this was refused, they sent messengers to all of the other factories in the district and the next day the strike was general.

During the strike, an effort on the part of strikers to prevent others from working, resulted in an encounter between strikers and the volunteer guards on duty at the factory. The results of this encounter were several persons killed and many wounded, among them an officer of the guard and several women and children. A judicial investigation was started by the Attorney General of the Republic in person but it seems that pressure was brought to bear on the local officials and the general manager and other high officials of the most important factory, with residence at Rio Blanco, where the encounter took place, were indicted, arrested and charged with having been seen to fire into the crowd of strikers. They were later released on bail. As they were French and their arrest occurred on the day before the French celebration of their national holiday, the French colony of Orizaba, as a protest, suspended all celebration of the day.

During former strikes the merchants of Orizaba have donated provisions for the strikers and their families, probably to prevent overt acts on the part of the strikers. This time, however, little, if anything, was given.

The federal government, through the recently created Bureau of Labor, made every possible effort to settle the strike. The managers of the factories, while willing to make some concessions to the demands of the laborers, finally threatened to close the factories for an indefinite period and to compel the men to vacate their residences, the property of the company, unless they would return to work within two days. The men finally went back to their work but found that many of them had been singled out and were refused further employment. The Bureau of Labor was unable to secure from the companies a reconsideration of this decision and it became necessary for them to take care of the men and their families until work could be secured elsewhere. An attempt was made by the government to solve the question by offering public land in the state of Chiapas free to those dissatisfied but, for lack of financial support, the men could not accept. While the trouble has been temporarily adjusted, the men are not satisfied and it is only a question of time till there is a fresh outbreak.

The corps of federal rurales in this state has headquarters in Orizaba. They should number over one thousand but their number is sometimes reduced to but a few men. They are under the command of Gen. Tapia. This man is a saddler by trade and before the last revolution lived in Orizaba. At the beginning of the revolt against the former administration he was suspected of implication and, to escape arrest, he disappeared. He was next heard of as a revolutionary leader and became famous for what he was supposed to have done for the revolution, but the fact is that he kept in hiding with friends in the mountains. A short time ago, after an altercation in a saloon, he shot at his opponent and killed an innocent bystander. He was arrested but soon released and now is again at the head of his command. His son, who is holding a commission under him, recently took advantage of the latter's absence to forge his father's name to a telegram in order to have a subordinate arrested and turned over to him. Within an hour after the prisoner was delivered to him, he shot him down on account of some old personal grudge. He afterward gave himself up to the authorities but is now out on bail and back at his post, although the act committed is not bailable according to Mex. Law.

One revolutionary leader who, a few months ago, surrendered to the authorities and was pardoned, is reported back in the field at the head of a small band of marauders. Just recently another leader, Panuncio Martinez, who has been marauding with his band between here and the mountains, accepted the offer of amnesty made to him by the federal government through special envoys. However, he surrendered with only 65 of his followers and a small number of arms. It is reported that other leaders in the districts near the Isthmus have surrendered. Personally I have no confidence in these transactions. Nothing prevents these men from returning to their outlawry. There are still several bands in the field and but last week a village on the Mexican Ry. 40 miles from Veracruz was assaulted and robbed.

Soon after the changes in the administration of the federal government, changes also took place in the state and city governments of Veracruz. Two or three persons were appointed to the so called provisional governorship of the state but before any of these successive appointees could take charge, the legislature, probably influenced by the threatening attitude of a body of rebels in the state capital, appointed another who immediately took charge. This man lasted but a few months. The dissatisfaction with his administration became so general that the federal government had to advise him to resign. To give more weight to the advice, a detachment of federal troops took possession of the government building "to prevent disorder". Then came the popular election of a governor to finish the legal term. The result of this election was that one of the candidates, who and whose partizans claimed the majority of votes but who was not declared elected by the state legislature, started a revolution. He was shortly afterwards made a prisoner and is still in the fortress of Ulua. During the term of office of the opponent, the election for the next legal term was held. There were many candidates. A short time before the election took place, the governor resigned "on account of ill health" (?). He has temporarily been succeeded by the chairman of the state legislature. In this election comparatively few people voted, it being considered useless. Results are not yet known. As the state legislature is the legal authority to decide who is elected, the impression prevails among the majority of the population and the same opinion is freely expressed in the press, that not the candidate who received the most votes will be declared governor. During this election for governor, several citizens of a small town in the northern part of the state, claiming their right to elect their own candidate, refused to vote as the Jefe Politico directed. They were taken out and summarily shot as an example to the rest of the population.

Under the first provisional governor, an election for new officials for this city was held. This was supposed to be the first opportunity of the people to enjoy the right of suffrage under the new regime and from 35 to 45% of the voters made use of their franchise. The successful candidates were however "Personas non gratas" with the government, and the election was annulled. Since then election for city officials were ordered twice; seven votes one time and less than fifty the other were the results; the impression of most of the people being that it was idle to vote for anyone not favored by the federal or state government. As a result, Veracruz, a city of fifty thousand inhabitants, is ruled by the same officials elected or appointed five or six years ago. It is doubtful whether their acts are legal.

Ever since the advent of the new administration, county and town or municipal officials throughout the state have been changed as often, or even oftener, as the governor; there having been abrogations in many cases of the appointments of officials even before they could take charge of their provisional offices. In other cases those appointed were not to the liking of the people and bloody encounters between citizens and officials resulted. The most recent case of the kind occurred just last week.

The same unsatisfactory conditions exist in the judicial branch of the government. The county of Veracruz has four county courts. For many months but one of them was administered by a member of the bar, the other three being in charge of laymen. The same conditions prevail in other counties. Naturally, in view of the foregoing, other branches of the government are in the same abnormal conditions, that most seriously affected being the treasury, both state and municipal. In a report of a special commission appointed by the state legislature, it appears that the cash reserve in the state treasury of over half a million was reduced during the administration of the first provisional governor to 147,000 pesos and that this same governor sent to the legislature an estimate of expenses, for the ensuing year, which exceeded that of the previous year by 35%. One instance will serve as an example of the use to which this money was put. Thirty six tons of print paper were purchased for use in the publication of the official state gazette. For this paper 22 cents per Kilogram (2.2 lbs.) was paid. The succeeding administration, finding that there was a large surplus of this paper, ordered its sale. The best offer received was 11 cents per Kilogram.

The Veracruz city treasury had about 125,000 pesos cash on hand at the time of the change of the administration of federal government. This surplus has been exhausted and at present they are unable to meet current expenses.

Upon the receipt of each letter, of which copy is enclosed herewith, a copy was forwarded to the Embassy. A copy of this despatch is now also transmitted.

I have the honor to be, Sir,

                              Your obedient servant,
                              (signed) Wm. W. Canada
                              Consul

Enclosures: Copies of 12 letters and despatch and enclosures in
              duplicate.

File 800.

Enclosure with Despatch No. 760, August 23, 1912.

AMERICAN CONSULAR SERVICE
Hacienda El Potrero, Veracruz

COPY   August 23, 1912

Hon. W. W. Canada,
      American Consul,
            Veracruz.

Dear Sir:

Owing to so many matters claiming attention yesterday, it was impossible to write confirming my personal interview of August 21. The general conditions which prevail here are truly deplorable -- since my return with Mrs. Lawrence on August 3. We have lived here quietly enough, but with full knowledge that there are some 200 armed bandits around us at all times, who, while as yet have not molested us, pass through our lands daily, and are committing depredations on adjoining places -- as well as at San Juan de la Punta, San Lorenzo, Paso del Macho, Camaron, Omealca, etc. -- not once but daily -- all within a radius of some 12 miles. We have had ten rurales -- Maderista soldiers stationed here since our return, but they are not adequate for the protection of the place. On the evening of August 20th, at 7:30 p.m., the captain of Rurales came to me stating that he had captured three spies who stated that we were to be raided that night, and we were advised by the captain to go away over night. We left at 9:30 p.m. on train for Cordoba, returning here on 5:30 a.m. train and wired for reinforcements, some 15 men being sent here during the afternoon. The captain again advised us that several hundred bandits were encamped in one of our forests within a mile of the factory and urged us to leave at 5:30 p.m. for Veracruz which we did for safety, and called on you, explaining all these conditions. It is quite true that so far no raids have been made on us, but from general information coming to us, this may be the case any day or night, so that our people, foreigners and natives, are quite demoralized, making it hard to keep employees or get our work done. In fact, since January 1st, 1912, we have been short over 350 men daily, as they will not work owing to the unsettled conditions, fearing both the bandits as well as being forced to military service by this government. We are now making repairs in factory, doing field work, as best we can, all of the which must be done in order to have any crop at all, taking in our needed supplies, all of which involve a cash expenditure of over 200,000 pesos between now and December 31st, so as to start our grinding season; so you can easily understand the hardship we labor under, not knowing whether we can go on, whether the place will be ruined, and whether when we reach the grinding we can secure labor to do our work, or can ever complete it. Our crop next season, starting January 1, 1913, will probably produce 800,000 pesos in four or five months, so you can see where we stand, and how hard all these times are for us, and others of the Americans in this State, working under same conditions. We need only tell you that our direct losses since January 1st, 1912, are fully 300,000 pesos, or more owing to the conditions described, and how much more will be -- who knows! The investment here is something over $2,000,000 Am. Cy., and we are suffering greatly in every way, not only financially, but peace of mind. What can we do? Where do we stand? What is the outlook? And, where is it all going to end? And, what is our government ever going to do, to make it safe to live and work in this country? Many Americans are wondering why they are so, if their government doesn't protect them -- so do I -- and I'm as good an American, who loves the flag and am ashamed of its course.

Yours truly,
(signed) Albert Lawrence.

Enclosure with Despatch No. 760, August 23, 1912.

AMERICAN CONSULAR SERVICE
Texonapa, Veracruz

COPY   August 2, 1912

Wm. W. Canada,
      U. S. Consul,
            Veracruz.

Dear Sir:

It has occurred to me that the following incident is a fit subject for the information of your Department though its immediate application in so far as the writer is concerned affects the El Palmar Estates, a British Company under my charge, the details of said incident now forming the subject of correspondence as between the writer and H.B.M. representative and up to the moment without solution.

While at El Palmar the other day we received a type-written communication from the home of Gonzales & Co. at Tezonapa, stating that they had been empowered by two representatives of the Mexican Government, giving names, to communicate with property owners in the neighborhood of Tezonapa, ourselves amongst the number, setting forth the following points - viz - that said two representatives of the Mexican Government had just returned from a conference with Panuncio Martinez, the Rebel leader of some two hundred armed and mounted men - said conference having been held at Acatlan - that this leader was ready to lay down his arms, also his followers being ready to do the same - under an agreement of amnesty with the Government - terms as follows - that he Panuncio Martinez would then form a corps of 25 of his best men, receiving from the Government arms and accoutrements - regular rural outfit - and prosecute a vigorous campaign against other offenders - the rest of his following to be disbanded - so far, so good enough - but carrying with it the astounding proposal that the sum of $4000 pesos must be provided by the suffering property owners to pay off the salaries due by P. Martinez to his followers as the Government declined to do so - that the house of Penagos of Cordoba - a wealthy concern - was to be the depositary of the funds collected winding up with the suggestion that this would be a fine thing to do and that no doubt the law-abiding haciendados and fingueros would respond promptly to so attractive a plan whereby peace and security of life and property would be assured. To this I sent a polite reply stating that I would take the matter up for immediate consideration, which I did with the British representative. I have not my copy by me, but this is about the gist of it. First, that we have no immediate means of knowing whether it is authoritative upon the part of the Government and meantime we must have an assurance through H. B. M. representative that it is authoritative, secondly that upon the part of my company a foreign corporation paying pretty stiff taxes and acting for them, I should certainly decline to be a party to a compromise as between the Mexican Government and its offenders - we paying the bill - by a direct contribution of blood money - further, that until I was duly advised by the authorities I should regard the proposals as impossible as emanating from the Mexican Government - that we, a foreign corporation who have already been compelled under duress to contribute a small sum to the Madero revolution, which by the way has not been refunded by the present Government as yet – and further that we were levied upon in the month of February by this same Panuncio Martinez and his gang of rebels 150 strong, armed and mounted, seems to the writer to be so odious a proposal that I decline to believe it possible as emanating from the Government and shall so report it until advised officially to the contrary.

While in Tezonapa yesterday awaiting the train to come in here, I learned that several Mexican and Spanish property owners had left the previous day for Cordoba to confer at the establishment of Penagos with reference to the raising of the sum of money already mentioned – from which it would appear that there must be some foundation for the letter received by us. I shall certainly hesitate to send such a report to a British Board of Directors. I make no comments but I fancy you will easily divine what my opinion is of such a set of proposals.

Very truly yours,
(signed) J. C. Harvey

Enclosure with Despatch No. 760, August 23, 1912.

AMERICAN CONSULAR SERVICE
Tezonapa, Veracruz

COPY   June 6, 1912

Wm. W. Canada, Esq.,
    U. S. Consul,
        Veracruz.

Dear Sir:

Since writing you yesterday in the hope that means might be found whereby my communication would promptly reach the Minister of Governacion in Mexico, I note in the public press the announcement of Mr. Wilson's departure for the United States, though possible this will make no difference. Of course I could write the Governor of the State, the local Jefe Politico or the Minister of Governacion, but frankness compels me to say I am a little tired of that sort of thing, since that course persued diligently since the latter part of February has brought no soldiers nor rurales on to any of the properties under my charges, unless such have been at Buena Ventura since June 3rd, date of the last advise received from there.

There is also another element that particularly adds to the complication at that Estate, viz: that for many years I have recruited my laborers for that property wholly in the village of Oluta, where we are well known and have the complete confidence of those indigenes - it being an Indian village - just and human treatment has invariably characterized our relations with them; full substantiation of this fact can be had by the Government should they desire to satisfy themselves of it. Now the point at issue is that the annual feast comes off shortly after the 15th current; and the custom demands that we go there to make arrangement with all those we may wish to re-employ or such as wish to return for another season; and if this source of terror be not promptly removed, we shall be unable to recruit our men in which event we shall be in still worse case.

Referring again to the man Antonio Pavon Gallegos, there should be no doubt whatever about this man's character; let the following suffice,-some years ago I gave him employment and he came with his family,-I helped him financially several times, in a fit of passion he cut his own daughter, a young woman of some sixteen years, with a matchete on arm and head. I washed and bound up her wounds and threatened to advise the authorities if he did not mend his ways, which he did for a time. Later, in some domestic difficulties in his house on the Estate, he took a five gallon tin of boiling water from the fire and threw it over his wife, an Indian woman, whose state for a fortnight or longer was indeed pitiable. I washed daily with my own hands her wounds, anointing them with proper medicaments. As soon after her recovery as possible I discharged this man, as such a fiend incarnate was not to be tolerated. This therefore is the man who instigates brigands' attack upon gringos. Does the Government desire to have proof of my statements before acting, I should like to know?

Now Mr. Canada, I sincerely trust you will find the way to press these details upon the ear of the Government. On rereading my letter I desire to clarify one statement which implies that communications have been sent to the Minister of Governacion at intervals since last February, this is not correct. The communications have been directed to the Government at Xalapa; also a special messenger was sent there upon one occasion. The only direct communication to the Minister of Governacion was sent June 2nd and to which no reply has been received as yet.

                                        Yours truly,
                                    (signed) J. C. Harvey

AMERICAN CONSULAR SERVICE
Tezonapa, Veracruz

COPY   June 5, 1912

Dear Mr. Canada:

I enclose the letters received from my people, illiterate enough it is true, but none the less reliable for all of that. I am in no frame of mind to back down if I can avoid it. These bandits could be easily cleaned out and no more salutary thing could be accomplished that their capture and proper treatment thereafter as a warning for others.

I now ask you to transmit these communications to the American Embassy without loss of time. My associates in California are besieging me with inquiries as to the situation at Buena Ventura. I see not the least reason why I should prevaricate, furthermore I have no stomach for these things.

I don't exactly know how best to get a certain sort of information I should like to give to the Government, but it is like this: if a corps of rurales be sent to nab Antonio Pavon Gallegos at his house on the hill back of Santa Rosa station, he can tell the whole thing, so the band can be cleaned out, that is certain and easy. There is no man living in Mexico, foreign or native, that has a greater respect for constituted authority than I, hence I conceive that I am doing a proper service in this matter notwithstanding my resolute determination not to be frightened away. I hope you will be able to find a way to communicate these news and suggestions to the proper quarters.

Very truly yours,
(signed) J. C. Harvey

Enclosure with Despatch No. 760, August 23, 1912.

AMERICAN CONSULAR SERVICE
Tezonapa, Veracruz

<u>COPY</u>   June 5th, 1912

Wm. W. Canada, Esq.,
    U. S. Consul,
        Veracruz, Mexico.

Dear Sir:

I have to acknowledge the receipt of your letter of the 3rd. Up to this date I have no information from our Bueno Ventura Estate of any rurales or soldiers having arrived there, although all authorities have been advised by me of the incident of the 26th ultimo. Under date of 2nd I have received two communications from my people at Buena Ventura situated one hour back from Santa Rosa station, these two letters are from good men that I have always trusted.

You will observe that one Antonio is referred to. Full name Antonio Pavon Gallegos, a thoroughly bad sort, this man resides at Santa Rosa station in a little house on the hill above and is the instigator of much of this trouble.

Our force has become terrorized and is now reduced to five men who are clamoring for succor and funds to go away to the village. My son or I will visit the Estate this week to see to the wants, risk or no risk - and I desire the statement to be one of record.

Ample advises have been given to the authorities and we have definite promises dating back for weeks, that assistance would be sent, nothing has been done, and I now desire to have a definite reply from the authorities as to whether or not such immediate action will be taken to clean out this small band. If it be impossible to do so aid us I then merely desire to know the fact that I may advise my connections to that effect and formerly abandon Buena Ventura, at least for the time being, as I have no intention to run away.

I have seven heads of riding animals on the place and I suppose these bandits covet them so they may continue their depredations – these they did not secure on the first visit – since the animals were running in a remote pasture.

Very truly yours,
(signed) J. C. Harvey

Two enclosures.

Enclosure with Despatch No. 760, August 23, 1912.

AMERICAN CONSULAR SERVICE
Buena Ventura

COPY   June 2, 1912

Sr. C. Harvey,
     My dear Sir:

     I have received your letter of the 1st instant asking me how many
people I now have. In reply I may state five including myself only
Matilde went away (after the attack), but the remaining ones say they
want to go away as they fear the bandits will return and kill them,
hence they are with reason alarmed.

     These bandits declare they are not bandits, yet they carried off
things enumerated. They expressed themselves that if I said anything
about this they would return and kill me; therefore I fear to remain
and wish to get away as quickly as possible, life is more valuable than
anything else. They go about during the night and I have heard firing
quite close.

                                        (signed)

(Free translation of the original in Spanish, made by Mr. Harvey.)

Enclosure with Despatch No. 760, August 23, 1912.

AMERICAN CONSULAR SERVICE
El Returo

COPY   June 2, 1912

Mr. C. M. Harvey,

    Dear Sir:

    I have just received your letter of yesterday and in reply will state that Cortez and the other man are still living in the other camp, going ahead as before, Matilde Molina was the only one that refused to obey the orders to remain. Regarding the list of things you ask about I find it impossible to state exactly, as I did not see them, but Juan informs me they (the bandits) carried off the following: 2 riding saddles, 4 or 5 blankets, boots and shoes, 1 rifle and some tinned provisions.

    I note that you propose to come here again but first let me say that Antonio is at the bottom of the trouble. He is in conspiracy with them and he it was that advised them.

    Also that three men connected with the band inquiring about our riding stock and further stated that Antonio told them about said riding stock.

                          (signed)

(Free translation of the original in Spanish, made by Mr. Harvey.)

Enclosure with Despatch No. 760, August 23, 1912.

AMERICAN CONSULAR SERVICE
Tatahuicapa, Veracruz

COPY   May 31, 1912

Mr. Wm. W. Canada,

U. S. Consul,

Veracruz, Mexico,

Dear Sir:

For more than a month past I have been very much under the weather, part of the time uncomfortably sick in bed, and the rest of the time barely crawling about, but am beginning to mend a little, and I hasten to advise you of events in this neighborhood during the past two or three weeks. It is quite likely you may know of them through Mr. Gould or Mr. Hill.

A month ago it was rumored that a band numbering anywhere from fifty to one hundred was encamped across the river from Playa Vicente awaiting a favorable opportunity to sack the place. They were next heard of in the vicinity of San Gabriel and Arroyo Tomate, where it was said they killed a man in the camino. Next we heard of them as being in Santa Cecilia and Sochiapa, settlements on the road leading from this place to Playa. It was said that several men were killed in these two places. Then they went into Playa and evidently did not meet with much opposition, for the federals had not yet arrived. Here they ousted the Alcalde and the Justice of Peace, and all the other officials installing a complete new set of their own, their chief, Santana Zavaleta, being the new Alcaldo. There have been various rumors more or less conflicting, as to what they did during their short reign in Playa. Some say they levied heavy contributions in money, others that there was not much money taken but plenty of cattle, horses, saddles, guns and ammunitions. It is probable that they did not miss any of these things within their reach. Among other things it is said that they imprisoned several of the prominent merchants, probably by way of pressure. All this time there was no open conflict.

Then presently un partido of their band, numbering about twenty five or thirty, came into this place, ten of them under the leadership of Santana coming to my place, on Sunday afternoon two weeks ago, demanding carabinas and saddles. They were about as gentlemanly as people bent on that mission could be, making no more fuss or disturbance than the score or more of their numbers have been making me during the past thirteen years. If there is any difference I must say it is in favor of Santana, who came frankly in broad daylight and asked for what he wanted, while the others all have operated under cover of the night, or when they have known I was away from home, and then everybody, even the local officials, have turned in and helped to protect them from discovery.

When I told them I had no gun of any sort or size, they were not inclined to believe me, and one of their number, evidently the second in command, said he would go into the house and see for himself. I went with him opening every cupboard, box, closet, or other possible hiding place, until he was satisfied I had told him the truth, and meanwhile Santana who remained outside helped himself to my best saddle, two bridles, and my fine matchette, all having a cost value of $52. We shook hands and I remarked to them that they must excuse me if I failed to ask them to come again.

In the Pueblo they gathered in a small amount of money and three or four carabinas, changed the local authority, and the next day left for Playa where they met the federal soldiers who had in the meantime arrived from Veracruz. The conflict that ensued must have been something of a surprise to the bandinos, for it was short, sharp and decisive. They are said to have lost 39 killed, while the federals did not lose a man. If 39 bandinos (and their sympathizers) were killed, I suspect this count must include those suspects who have since been shot in the roads, for there have been quite a number of these.

The brigands scattered in various directions, some of them passing through this place, camping in this vicinity a few days, and others passing beyond in the direction of Trinidad, and the aftermath is now being gathered in. Unquestionably the brigands received aid and comfort from some of the people of this pueblo, and the stories are just leaking out, with the result that three of the most prominent persons of the place were arrested last night, and this morning left under strong escort for Playa to face the serious charges. There are others against whom quite as serious charges are pending, and they will in all probability have to travel the same route. You know very well that I have never been a sympathizer with the Government of Diaz, but I have no hesitation in saying that this method of dealing with this class of people was the only correct one under the circumstances, and brigandage can be stamped out only by the present Government pursuing the same course. The sunrise greeting against the adobe wall has a wonderfully deterring effect.

A very serious charge came to this place last night against two of the leading men of Trinidad, that they are harboring and aiding the bandinos in their preparations for another raid upon this place and Playa Vicento, and this communication has already been hastened on its way to the chief federal officer (Captain or Colonel) in Playa, and it is expected that there may be another clash before long not very far from here, or possibly in Playa.

In the meantime I am not well enough to make the trip to Playa (the only way of escape) even if I wanted to do so and I am not sure that I would be any safer anywhere between here and Veracruz than I am in my own house. I have never been a noisy individual anywhere, am known in all this region as strictly a non-combatant, and when I have traveled the Playa road, even at night and alone, have never carried a gun or a pistol. I have only a few head of horses and cattle, and but a very small amount of money, not much of a carcass to tempt the buzzards, and so far there has been no disposition to molest me even in these. My present feeling is that in my present state of health it is out of the question my getting out of the country.

In due time I expect of course to ask reimbursement for the saddle, bridles and machete, and would thank you to advise me as to the manner of proceeding. Should the account be sent to you, or to the Ambassador? And what verification will be necessary.

If there are further developments I shall hasten to advise you.

Yours very sincerely,
(signed) E. G. Church

Enclosure with Despatch No. 760, August 23, 1912.

AMERICAN CONSULAR SERVICE

Hda. "La Esmeralda", Paso del Cura, Veracruz

COPY   May 30, 1912

Mr. W. W. Canada,
        Consul,
                Veracruz, Mexico.

Dear Mr. Canada:

Upon my return to the place last week, I found that some days before the band of alleged rebels that had been holding out at Playa Vicente had made the place a visit, as they had done all the others, taking with them all our contract labor, some horses and merchandise, promising to return again for the liquidations of the labor, and to get the balance of the horses that were hidden in the woods.

In this they were forestalled by the appearance upon the scene of some 50 men of the 17th Regiment that killed some thirty odd, wounding many, most of whom escaped, and capturing a number of prisoners, some of whom have since been sent to V. C. The larger part of the party and all but the principal and possibly one other leader of the party escaped in the confusion to the mountains. They had committed all classes of depredations, and were daily growing worse. As a result of the taking of the labor from "La Estancia", Mr. Hill's place, when burning a small piece of clearing, the wind carried the fire to a piece of rubber and before it could be cut off by the natives that were called in until the next day, 225 acres of beautiful 4 year rubber was burned.

While in Playa a couple of days ago, I learned that the remainder of the rurales are to be taken away. In the name of the American interests of this vicinity, most of which at the present is without representation, I would ask that you communicate the matter to the

Ambassador, with the request that he use his influence with the Minister of Governacion to secure a permanent squad of from 15 to 20 mounted rurales for Playa Vicente. As without a guard the region is sure to be again the scene of "rebel" outrages that will eclipse the recent ones. The former band counts with a fair number of sympathizers that live in the town, and who in an unguarded moment might start the ball to rolling again, and if it begins, there is sure to be foreigners' blood in the streets.

I learn that Mr. E. G. Church of Tatahuicapa is seriously ill, with no one to care for him. I have written him asking if I can be of service, but as yet have not had time to receive a reply. Have you heard from him? He lives near the head of the Colorado river about 12 hours ride from here, and in case of serious illness should be removed by river to Juanita.

If I can be of service to you in any way, will be glad to attend to your instructions.

Awaiting your always welcome letters, with anything of interest that you may have to advise, I repeat myself at your orders and remain

most sincerely yours,
(signed) Leroy H. Ault

Enclosure with Despatch No. 760, August 23, 1912.

AMERICAN CONSULAR SERVICE
Sanborn, Vera Cruz, Mexico.

COPY   May 29, 1912

W. W. Canada, Esq.,
    U. S. Consul,
        Vera Cruz.

Dear Sir:

This is to advise you that a band of 20 bandits rode into our Buena Ventura Estate, a Los Angeles Company, an hour from Santa Rosa Station, back from the track of the V. C. al I. R. R. and six kilometers from Sanborn, breaking into our house and taking anything they thought might be useful, maltreating my people, men, and I am sorry to say, the women also. The incident occurred on the night of the 26th current. We realized some time ago that that locality was not safe, so visit them occasionally, in fact we were in the place on the 25th.

Now as regards running away I am a damned poor runner and while I propose to be prudent about my movements I am not the man to abandon either my own property nor that of others placed in my charge while a sporting chance remains. I have written a good many letters to the authorities both as affecting the British and American interests in my care, as long ago as the end of March when the first entrance was made at El Palmar. The Jalapa authorities were advised and some correspondence was had with the British and the Mexican Minister of Foreign Relations. Assurances were given that troops or rurales would be sent, they were not. Later, as it got hot down Buena Ventura way I sent a trusty emissary to Xalapa to detail "viva voce" certain facts which might facilitate matters, flattering promises were extended of immediate action -- but nothing came of it, -- and though I ought to have known better I was let into a fool's paradise for the time and now we have the consequences. If I could shake the dust of Mexico from my feet even if with some pecuniary loss, I would not require any advice whatever upon the subject -- as it is, my interests are unfortunately too great -- unless fairly driven out.

In a letter just written to the Governor of Vera Cruz I have advised him of the incident above mentioned and politely reminded him of the various communications without result - but in this instance I have abstained from any request for help which fact I hope he will observe and draw his own conclusions. The fact is, Mr. Canada, and I don't disguise it, we that remain don't look for any effective help from any source whatever and it ought to be a warning to both Britains and Americans to keep out of most Latin American countries -- would that I had never come here, however that regret is now too late.

Yours truly,
(signed) J. C. Harvey

Enclosure with Despatch No. 760, August 23, 1912.

AMERICAN CONSULAR SERVICE
Medina, Oaxaca, Mexico

COPY   May 28, 1912

Mr. Wm. W. Canada,
    American Consul,
        Veracruz, Ver.

Dear Sir:

I wired you this A.M. as follows: "Bandits raided Medina last night. Expect return. Arrange send rurales".

Yesterday morning we were informed that a small bunch of bandits about one-half mile from town and tried all day to get some rurales sent here but could not. About dusk 5 came in and they were watching for them at the store and when they came up captured the leader when the rest got away though they shot at them several times. Since there is quite a body of them about 10 miles away we were afraid they would come back so our people kept watch all night. The captured man proves to be a deserter from the rurales at Tierra Blanca.

I hope some rurales can be gotten here today to take charge and relieve our people. Also will you kindly use your influence to have a few rurales or soldiers stationed here for a few weeks for the protection of our people and take charge of matters or there will be a stampede from here.

Hoping you can arrange this at once, I remain

Yours truly,
(signed) G. N. Grigsby

Enclosure with Despatch No. 760, August 23, 1912.

AMERICAN CONSULAR SERVICE
Jalapa, Veracruz

COPY   May 27, 1912

Wm. W. Canada, Esq.,
    American Consul,
        Veracruz.

Dear Sir:

Attached find a copy of letters referring to a raid made on our Ranch "El Chaparral" on the 8th of the present month. I understand the revolutionists gave values for the things taken but have not as yet received any additional details. On receipt of more definite information will notify you.

On receipt of these letters we notified the Governor and despite his assurance of immediate steps being taken to apprehend said revolutionists, nothing effective has been done. Will keep you posted of future developments.

Yours very truly,
(signed) W. K. Boone

Enclosure with Despatch No. 760, August 23, 1912.

AMERICAN CONSULAR SERVICE
Plan de las Hayas, Veracruz

COPY   May 22, 1912

Mr. W. K. Boone,
    Jalapa.

Dear Sir:

I am replying to your favor of the 11th instant. On Friday last week I went to Juchique de Ferrer, stopping at the Ranch of Domingo Sayago. When at his place I received notice that the rebels had taken the village of Plan de las Hayas, exacting horses, arms and ammunition and money, and then had left for Juchique. There upon I went to Chaparral late in the evening thinking that this band would not enter the place. The next day, on Saturday, at about 8:30 p.m. they however arrived and behaved in a very violent manner, taking rifles, ammunition, a horse with its saddle, etc., but what they most desired was money. They searched for it everywhere; furniture, beds, etc., throwing about documents, papers, etc. They also cut the telephone wire. As they did not find the manager, they proceeded to the Sta. Teresa Ranch, where they committed the same acts of violence, but making a special search for the manager of the Chaparral hacienda, as they supposed that he had a large amount of money in his possession. Fortunately we both, the manager and myself, succeeded in escaping, taking with us the horses of the hacienda. When the bandits left they threatened to return, as they would not believe that no money was kept on hand in these haciendas.

(signed)

(Free translation.)

Enclosure with Despatch No. 760, August 23, 1912.

AMERICAN CONSULAR SERVICE
Tierra Blanca, Veracruz

COPY   May 15, 1912

Mr. Wm. W. Canada,
        American Consul,
                Veracruz, Ver.

Dear Sir:

Yours of the 14th inst. received. I thought in answer that I would
report conditions here and perhaps give you some news. So far as we
are concerned we have not been disturbed lately, but this part of the
country is still infested with "Bandits" and hardly a day passes that we
don't hear of them.

On the 4th of March, 38 of them called on us. Last Monday noon
this same gang, but numbering about 200 this time, rode within a mile
of Tierra Blanca and after terrorizing everybody and causing the few
rurales and soldiers stationed there to become panic stricken, passed on
North without entering the town.

The soldiers were sure badly scared. They hardly knew what they
were about and were running this way and that, and yelling at each
other. They finally concluded that if they had horses they might make
their escape, so they pressed in all the horses they could find and
when properly mounted rode off in a good safe direction. They took one
of our horses and a new saddle that happened to be in town, but we
got them back today.

Six of the bandits came out to see us and look the situation over.
They captured our store keeper at the river and made him come back
with them and open the store. They said their Jefe had given them

orders to behave themselves at the Joliet and that if they wanted anything at the store to pay for it, which they started in to do, but they were a little boozzie [sic] and all began clamoring for stuff at the same time and the store keeper says they may have got away without paying for all the beer they drank. They were quite nervous while here and when they called on some of our women for something to eat they sat on their horses all the time and kept a sharp look out.

When they left our Mayordomo went with them a short distance to show them the road out. They were just drunk enough to talk freely and told him that while they were quiet in passing here, they raised "Hell" at other places and to make their word good, when they reached El Carmen they were in condition for anything and called on a Mexican. His family hid in the brush while they tied and threatened to kill him, but did nothing more than rob him of what money he had. He sent his family to Veracruz today for safety.

This is rather a long story, but facts and I thought you might be interested enough to read it.

Respectfully yours,
Joliet Tropical Plantation Co.
(signed) J. C. Dennis

Enclosure with Despatch No. 760, August 23, 1912.

AMERICAN CONSULAR SERVICE
Tierra Blanca, Ver.

COPY   May 21, 1912

Mr. Wm. W. Canada,
        American Consul,
              Vera Cruz, Mex.

Dear Sir:

Last week we located our old gang of bandits. We found they had not gone far and still had our pay roll in mind. Last Sunday we called on the authorities in Tierra Blanca for help to run them down and they agreed to send a bunch of rurales out Tuesday (today) morning.

I am glad to say that they did send four and we reinforced their number with three of our best men, men that we could illy afford to lose in a fight. The rurales showed up at 3 A.M. and all were ready to start the hunt at 3:30, but you know it is a long time from Sunday until Tuesday -- plenty of time for the gang to get word to look out for themselves, which they did. But our men made a thorough search and found evidence in many places of where the thieves had just left. They probably were under cover in the brush and may be are back doing business at the old stand by this time.

The Jefe of the rurales was very much interested and says he will not give up the fight and may get them yet.

Otherwise conditions are about the same as when we last reported.

                            Respectfully yours,
                            Joliet Tropical Plantation Co.
                            (signed) J. C. Dennis

Enclosure with Despatch No. 760, August 23, 1912.

AMERICAN CONSULAR SERVICE
Tierra Blanca, Ver.

COPY   May 13, 1912.

Mr. Wm. W. Canada,
        American Consul,
            Veracruz, Ver.

Dear Sir:

I hereby make report to you of conditions here. The Governor of Veracruz paid attention to us so far as to send 25 soldiers to Tierra Blanca who reached there last Thursday. They were not very anxious to come out to our place and finally put off coming until Friday as they understood that Oaxaca was to send a force to take care of us. In the meantime if we had any trouble, we were to let them know.

At 4 o'clock p.m., Friday, 20 soldiers from Tuxtepec did come out to our place and we made all arrangements with them for rations. We furnished rice, beans, and we at once gave them a hog for meat and everything seemed lovely, but about 4 p.m., Saturday they received orders to go somewhere else and did so at once, and now so far as the authorities are concerned we are in the same conditions we have been all along. The first gang of robbers who were camped on the Yale so long have decamped for parts unknown, but we learned yesterday that another gang had been camped on our own place, but understand now that they also have moved on.

Thanking you most hardly for your efforts in our behalf, I am

                                Sincerely yours,
                        La Joliet Tropical Plantation Co.
                            (signed) J. C. Dennis

CIA. CONSTRUCTORA DE FERROCARRILES, S. A.

Patzcuara
September 4, 1912

Mr. Arnold Shanklin,
    Consul General,
        Mexico, D. F.

Dear Sir:

Acknowledging receipt of yours of Sept. 4th, I am glad to furnish you any information as to conditions in this section of the country which may come to my knowledge. Well, the situation may be summed up in a very few words. The country is in a state bordering on anarchy. With the exception of a few of the more important towns, where they have soldiers, whose duties are apparently to guard the government officials, the whole of the rural districts are entirely at the mercy of the bandits. They go and come as they please robbing, looting and committing acts of brutality till they have either become too intoxicated to continue or until even their brute natures have become satiated. In the rural districts there is absolutely no protection for foreigners of Mexicans. As you know this country is an Indian district, and these Indians either have or imagine that they have a grievance coming on account of lands which they consider that they have been robbed of. Every one who has a grievance coming to him joins the Zapatistas and in the unprotected condition of the country is at perfect liberty to settle his personal difficulties with his enemy. As regards our work on the construction of the Penjamo Ajuno line, if a Mexican foreman or Cabo is reproved for slack work, he either quits and joins the bandits, or advises some of his bandido friends to fix the man responsible for his insult. If a time keeper is discharged for being dishonest, he immediately becomes a general in the Zapatista army lays for his man. On the line from kilometer 75 to Ajuna, there are employed by the Railroad Company and by the Contracting Company, 150 foremen, engineers, superintendents of sub-contractors, 15 Americans, and 4

British subjects each one of whom is carrying his life in his hands with absolutely no protection from the Government. In this district during the past 6 or 8 months there have been 6 foreigners murdered and absolutely nothing done by the authorities to apprehend the murderers. The authorities feel themselves more or less secure with their soldiers, and do not care to have these soldiers leave the town in which they are located to chase bandits or murderers and then they are not over zealous in having a criminal apprehended or prosecuted, not caring to make enemies. I have tried diligently to find out if anything had been done towards apprehending the murderers of Mr. Ayres, I can find out absolutely nothing and it is my impression that absolutely nothing has been done, and it is my belief that nothing will ever be done unless the U. S. Government takes hold of the matter in such a vigorous manner as to force matters.

You understand that the elements of danger here are somewhat different from those in the North. While in the North there is a more or less organized revolution and the danger to foreigners there may result from battles or occupation of towns by revolutionary forces, here the danger, which is a constant one, comes from the absolute lack of law or rather of the enforcement of same, combined with the Indian element and the resultant acts of revenge or of pure savagery.

While the company I am working for is a Mexican one, and I do not feel under any obligation to them I have stayed on hoping that conditions would improve but they are very fast growing more serious and I have come to the conclusion that a man is a d---d jack ass to remain in Mexico under the present conditions and I think really all employees in Mexico would feel greatly relieved if the U. S. Government would order them out of the country.

The government cannot but know of the danger that all Americans are in in this country, and especially those in the rural districts, infested by bandits, whether the government can remedy matters or not I do not know, but unless I change my mind in a very short time I am going to pull out. Last night our Camp at Ajuna was raided by a band of 120 bandits and robbed of everything, the American foreman being held up at point of rifle and robbed of all his personal effects, being entertained while the robbery was going on with a tirade against the gringo. The authorities here and at Morelia knew of the movements of this band and although they had soldiers here in Patzcuara no effort was made to go after them or to head them off in their work of robbery. This is how we are fixed here and there is absolutely no use to ask for protection for we will not get it. The only protection to any American is to get out of Mexico.

Respectfully,
(signed) J. W. Anderson

C.H.I.B.

Customs Agency

****

FERROCARRILES NACIONALES DE MEXICO.

Eagle Pass Route

Apartado No. 21,

Piedras Negras, Coahuila, Mexico.

September 9, 1912

Hon. William H. Taft

    President of United States,

        Washington, D. C.

Sir:

The San Antonio papers of the 8th state that intervention is nearer now than ever; that conditions are growing worse in Mexico. No one should be better informed as to actual conditions in this republic than you are through the consular reports to the state department, at least if the facts as given by them to Mr. Knox are truthfully given to you.

I am in business communication with people from one end of the country to the other: Americans, English, Spanish, German, French and Chinese. I talk daily with men and women from Chihuahua to the City of Mexico and from the Gulf to the Pacific. I have asked many of them about intervention and they speak quickly and emphatically, "No! No! Never." The foreigners living in Mexico to a man are opposed to it. Those who have left the country are returning by every train, not only to the undisturbed districts, but to those localities recently held by rebels. Those returning are doing so at the request of their friends and relatives who remained behind, which is ample proof that there is some degree of safety for foreigners in the republic.

No bodily harm has befallen foreigners at the hands of the rebels, and those who remained were just as safe as those who flew out of the country; and the fact that those who remained were <u>not one of them harmed</u>, excepting one murdered colonist, stands uncontradicted today either thru consular reports, telegrams to the press or verbal messages from the traveling public.

Intervention is only talked of by those living out of the country, who have nothing to lose and everything to gain. Not one of them would take a hand to help you out; they are dollar-chasers and nothing else.

The better classes in Mexico will not lift a hand to put the rebellion down; they are too good for targets. What I call the better classes is from the merchant up. The rebellion is in the hands of the non-responsible classes, and there it will remain until starved out. The better classes will have nothing to do with it, either for or against, except a few would-be presidents, and that would be the stand taken by them if intervention should eventually come, in which event you would have to blockade their ports and seacoast line and frontier for contraband of war. Why not do it now? Cut off the guns and ammunition of the insurrectos, thus destroying their effectiveness, enabling the Mexican Government to better cope with them.

Better to guard their coasts and frontier and pay every damage claim presented than have one month of intervention. If the responsible classes in the republic will not turn out to keep the rabble from killing each other, it ought not to devolve on the United States to do so.

Guard their coast line and frontier against the introduction of war material as closely without intervention as you would have to do with intervention, and you will soon see a change in present conditions.

The government has but moderate facilities for the manufacture of ammunition, and the rebels none. Cut off their supply and they will stop. Don't jeopardize the lives of 150,000 to 200,000 of the best young men of the United States to suppress a rabble that the better class of Mexico, with ample facilities of means and men, refuse to put down.

Until the foreigners living in this country ask for intervention, corroborated by the consular service, for God's sake don't permit it. If you or Congress are bent on a high-handed history-making episode, blockade them fore and aft. Cut off the rebel's supply. They are not butchering each other with knives, but with bullets. Take these from them, and the government with its facilities for securing war supplies, will soon be able to suppress them.

I have lived in this country thirty years; read and write their language and know them. I offer my services to you if needed. I have had some correspondence with Major General Wood (personal friend) ever since the troubles in Mexico began, but have not communicated with him for some time, as conditions seemed to be running below normal, with nothing to report.

Please do not use my name in connection with this letter.

Yours respectfully,
(signed) J. N. Shafter

Address: P. O. Box 196,
            Eagle Pass, Texas.

COMMERCIAL REPRESENTATIVE OF THE MEXICAN GOVERNMENT
HERIBERTO BARRON
#102 West 32nd Street
New York, New York

September 12, 1912

Hon. William Howard Taft,
    President of the United States of America,
        Beverley, Mass.

Your Excellency:

Having greeted you with every expression of my personal respect, permit me to convey to you like greetings from the International Committee of Peace and Amity of Mexico City, which Committee deeply appreciative of your beneficent co-operation in its work of establishing a lasting fraternal peace between our two countries, has placed in my hands for presentation to you their autograph expression thereof.

This letter, together with a portrait group of the said Committee, I shall deliver to you, in person, at such time as it may be your Excellency's pleasure to appoint.

It is with profoundest gratitude and deepest appreciation that I, that all patriotic Mexicans welcome your public denouncement of the recent persistent efforts to force upon or to make you appear to favor and to be about to precipitate the military invasion of Mexico.

Despite all the inflammatory statements on the subject that have recently appeared in the press, and that would seem to convey impression of your intention to intervene in Mexican internal affairs, I, together with all Mexicans and Americans residing in Mexico and conversant with your course throughout, believe implicitly in the sincerity of your friendship for Mexico and in your unimpeachable justice of nature and incapability of betraying our trust in you.

Your splendid telegram to the International Committee of Peace and Amity on the occasion of the Mexican-American meeting in Mexico City on July 4th last, in the interest of friendly peace between the two countries, made a pacific and grateful impression upon the hearts of the Mexican people; indeed your every act and word through the recent Mexican disturbances has created the universal impression in Mexico that you and your great Nation are true friends of Mexico; that you would help, not harm us in the struggle to restore peace and order and to entrench upon firm foundation legal constitutional government in the Republic.

But we well know how the intendedly spectacular acts of disorganized, tottering insurrection, seeking to save its face through the accomplishment of an intervention might impose upon a wide-awake press eager for news, an entirely distorted view of the real situation, and for a time, at least, divert public attention for the steady progress of the government in its crushing of destructive revolt.

The very fact that Mexican insurrectionaries are willing to resort to such methods as would seem to invite intervention, is in itself proof of the successful energy of the Constitutional government in its suppression of lawless revolt.

Naturally deceived by what at first is made to appear the real situation, it is far from surprising that many here, having friends and interests in Mexico, in the first moment of the indignation caused by inflammatory news should fall discussing in the heat of the moment, the advisability of a war.

But may the God of Nations ever prevent the taking of so serious a step - upon the impulse of momentary excited indignation, with no proper consideration of whether the cause thereof was well established, with no definite certainty that the justness of the principle involved was so great that it became necessary to set two peoples killing each other, thereby multiplying a thousandfold the loss of life, the misery that has already been suffered.

Such a war would be not merely unjustified by the facts as we see them, but inexpressibly unfortunate.

It would irreparably wreck the best present common interests of both countries.

It could not be, even under most favorable circumstances, other than a prolonged destructive conflict, productive of wide spread international complications and fraught with great loss of life, of commerce and to us possibly of our autonomy.

To you it could not but result in loss of the trust and confidence of the Latin-Americas and your own National pre-eminently high place among modern nations, for international Justice and Honor.

Therefore, Mr. President, your vigorous public statement of your unalterable determination to permit no pressure to divert you from your attitude of amity toward Mexico, is of itself, of immense weight in counteracting the efforts of those seeking to stir the countries to the verge of war. And accept my assurance that in Mexico all is being done by the President and patriots of the country toward the same end.

In behalf of all patriotic Mexicans, from the depths of my heart, I beg to thank you for your great and brave stand in the present grave crisis.

I have, Sir, the honor to be,

With every expression of respect,

Your obedient servant,

(signed) Heriberto Barron

P. S.   Believing as I do, that the publication of the above letter together with your reply thereto, will be most effective for the welfare of both Mexico and the United States and will be highly appreciated by the public of both Nations, I respectfully beg you, Mr. President, if you have no objections, to make my letter public as well as your reply thereto, and also to grant to me permission to publish both letters.

(signed) H. B.

*   *   *   *   *   *   *

Cumeral, Sonora, Mexico.
September 20th, 1912.

Mr. Thomas D. Bowman,
       American Vice Consul in Charge,
             Nogales, Sonora.

Dear Sir:

You are advised that on Sept. 12th Emilio Campa, rebel bandit leader, entered the Cerro de Plata Mining Camp of which I am Superintendent and Principal owner, looted our store, insulted the American employees and drove off twenty-two head of animals.

A few days previous I wrote Mr. Louis Hostetter American Consul at Hermosillo that our camp was in danger and requested that he send us arms and ammunition for protection. Consequently he sent us fifteen rifles and seventeen hundred cartridges which arrived at our station, Cumeral, fifteen miles distant on the 9th of Sept. and the next day our stage brought out ten rifles and all of the cartridges, leaving five rifles at the station. As Campa was then reported near Cananea we did not make arrangements to put out guards, but decided to organize our men into a company and patrol the camp a few days later, depending somewhat on rumor as to the whereabouts of robber bands. On the 12th our stage again started for Cumeral to get the mail and bring out the other five rifles. About three miles from camp the stage met Campa's advance guard consisting of seven men. The guard held up the stage but allowed it to proceed, as there was nothing of value aboard. On reaching the railroad our driver met Colonel Camberos with 130 Federal soldiers and told him the rebels were only three hours away. Camberos refused to follow them giving as excuse that he had come up to see about the bridges Campa had burned the day previously.

As for myself I was at the mine when the rebels entered our camp directing the building of a tramway. At ten thirty A.M. one of our policemen came running up the trail and told me the camp had been taken by surprise and that the rebels were hunting me and the Comisario because we had arranged to defend the camp. He said the Comisario had hidden and that I had better skip or they would kill me on sight. As I was unarmed and as the camp had been taken I was forced to follow his advice so I started out afoot traveling west through the mountains toward the Alamo Ranch. Late in the afternoon I came to a ranch, secured a horse and got to the Alamo at nine P.M. A little later Mr. Beckford Kibby came in saying that the rebels had held up a roundup fifteen miles to the north and disarmed thirty cowboys taking their horses and saddles. He also stated that he and six of his men were at the time repairing a fence nearby but hearing of the rebels in time they all managed to escape. At the Alamo there were three other Americans besides Mr. Kibby and myself, also six cowboys. All hands were well armed. We expected the rebels in the next morning and we expected to make a stand against them, but they did not show up, instead they went to Saric on the Altar river and later to Tubutama and Altar capturing and looting these places. At Altar they killed a number of citizens.

On the morning of the thirteenth I secured a horse guide and guns from Mr. Kibby and returned to the mine arriving late in the afternoon and found most of my men still at camp but the rebels were all gone. My American employees consisted of Mr. Arcus Reddock the bookkeeper, Mr. Charles Wilkie the millwright, and Mr. L. C. Morrow Assayer. On reaching camp I was told that Campa looted the place the day before shortly after I had left, taking about $3000.00 Mex. in goods from the store and about twenty-two head of animals. When he found that we had made arrangements for a defense he became very angry and gave Mr. Reddock fifteen minutes to show him where I was hidden, saying he would hang him to a tree if he failed to do as he was told. Mr. Reddock finally convinced him that he did not know where I was so Campa then had a squad of rebels then march him to the mine looking for me. At the mine the rebels ran across Mr. Wilkie and Mr. Morrow whom they abused in the vilest manner, threatening also to hang them if they refused to reveal my hiding place. Finally the three Americans were marched back to the store where they were again threatened and abused. Later the gang left going west.

Am glad to say that while we are employing about one hundred men, only five of them left with Campa and two of these were Manchurians. So it is evident from this and the little headway that Campa has made recruiting in Northern Sonora at the various points he has visited that the people of this state are not in favor of the revolutionary movement.

After arranging for work to continue I rode into Imuris on the 14th and found Colonel Camberos still making preparations to follow the bandits and two days later he succeeded in getting away from the railroad at Santa Ana but arrived in Altar after that town had been plundered and a number of citizens killed as stated above, so it is plain that Camberos could have beaten the rebels to Altar thirty hours if he had left the railroad in time.

And right here I wish to say the main trouble with the Federal army is about half of the Commanders are absolutely N. G. On the other hand the rank and file are good fighters. I wish to say however that there are a few good Federal leaders in the field, among these are Colonel Giron, who is now giving Campa a hard chase, Colonel Obregon, operating below Douglas and Colonel Kosterlitzky, who has just returned from Mexico City and is now organizing three hundred picked men. From what I know of the Colonel something will be going as soon as he gets into the field. Such men as these are a credit to Mexico and if the Federal Authorities will weed out the incompetent leaders, I believe the revolution will soon be wiped out in Sonora. The only danger now seems to lie in the fact that all the rebel leaders are threatening to kill American Citizens because the United States Government gave Mexico permission to pass troops through American territory. I understand this threat is quite general.

As to our claim for the goods and chattles taken away from us will say that we will later render you an itemized statement concerning same signed by several witnesses.

Truly yours,
(signed) E. B. Holt

AMERICAN CONSULATE

Tampico, Mexico

No. 654   November 3, 1912

SUBJECT: Political Conditions.

The Honorable

    The Secretary of State,

        Washington.

Sir:

Referring to my despatch number 625 of Oct. 22nd, last, I have the honor to report further as follows, viz.:

On October 23rd, it was reported from the oil camps in Northern Vera Cruz that the revolutionists were moving north with Tampico as the objective point. The following day it was rumored in this city that Vera Cruz had been retaken by the Government forces. The revolutionists apparently heard the same report because they ceased their march to the north and went back toward Tantima and Amatlan. The various bands continued marching back and forth demanding and receiving from the various oil camps money, provisions, horses, etc. They did not succeed in securing arms from these camps as they absolutely refused to surrender them.

On Oct. 22nd, this office was advised by the Embassy that the U.S.S. Tacoma would arrive about Oct. 24th, and I so notified the local officials who were more than pleased to receive the news. On Oct. 25th, the Tacoma arrived. The feeling of the local officials was shown by their remarks to me when I advised them of the probable arrival of the Tacoma - the Presidente Municipal and the Jefe de las Armas stated that that "was the best news which they could have received - the presence of the Tacoma would insure the preservation of order." The arrival of the Tacoma is thought to have had some bearing on the retirement of the revolutionists from the vicinity of Tampico.

The revolutionists continued to make their demands upon the camps of the foreign oil companies. These companies did not dare to refuse because of the great amount of property which the rebels could easily destroy if they so desired. However, these depredations grew burdensome and the representative of the Huasteca Petroleum Company (Doheny concern) on October 27th, wrote this office a letter asking that Capt. Durell of the Tacoma be requested to deliver to the company about 20 rifles. The Tacoma was not supplied in such a manner that this could be done so permission was not sought for this purpose. However, on the following day I wired the Embassy and the Governor of the State of Vera Cruz to the effect that these depredations of alleged revolutionists were becoming burdensome and unbearable and requesting that prompt and energetic measures be taken for the suppression of this lawlessness. A favorable reply was received from the Governor of the State and on Oct. 31st, the Mexican Gunboat Bravo arrived in port with 300 soldiers. These were sent for the special purpose of putting down this lawlessness and affording protection to the oil companies. Prior to this time no soldiers had been sent into this district as the local Jefe de las Armas had no troops to spare and his jurisdiction did not extend across the river. Absolutely no effort had been made by the Government to place troops in that district prior to this time. With the coming of the troops the bands of revolutionists began to disperse and according to best information obtainable practically all of them have dispersed. Some of the secondary leaders have surrendered. The Government is in control of Tuxpam and Ozuluama and practically the entire district. The revolution crumbled away almost as quickly as it came into existence. The troops now in the district are regarded as sufficient to give ample protection to the foreigners and foreign interests.

If General Diaz had been able to hold the advantage gained by his first success there is very little doubt but that the State of Tamaulipas would quickly have followed the example of Northern Vera Cruz. It is said that plans had been completed for the taking of Victoria, the State Capital, and that no resistance would have been encountered. If General Diaz had held Vera Cruz and the Mexican Government had not sent additional forces into Tampico and the <u>Tacoma</u> had not arrived, Tampico would have surrendered without much of a struggle.

In a sense the public is glad that the revolution failed. To be more correct the public is glad that the revolution failed so quickly if it could not succeed. There is a general feeling of regret that it did not succeed as quickly as it failed because the public hoped that its success would mean permanent peace. It is safe to state that the people of this district are for peace more than they are in favor of any individual.

Mr. A. C. Payne, the American Consular Agent in Tuxpam, who is General Manager of the Oil Fields of Mexico Co., together with Mr. Percy Furber, the President of the Company, were compelled at the points of loaded rifles to allow the rebels take a private train of the company from the station at Cobos across the Tuxpam River from Tuxpam. The War Commission in Tuxpam compelled the managers of the branches of the Tamaulipas & Vera Cruz Banks to deliver up $90,000 Mexican. They compelled the Collector of Customs at Tuxpam to deliver up all of the money in his charge. They prohibited people from passing in and out of Tuxpam. The treatment of Consular Agent Payne was brought to the attention of the Embassy and the Bravo landed fifty soldiers at Tuxpam on their way to Tampico on Oct. 30, 1912.

The only disturbance reported in the State of Tamaulipas was a raid of outlaws at Tula. This was of little importance, according to the information obtainable. However, such raids are not unusual in that section but there are very few Americans or other foreigners in that section according to the information in possession of this office.

Conditions appear to be normal and appear to justify my departure on my leave of absence within a few days. I shall wait until the arrival of the collier <u>Brutus</u> with coal for the <u>Tacoma</u> which is still in port. The Mexican Gunboat <u>Bravo</u> left at noon today for Vera Cruz.

I have the honor to be, Sir,

> Your obedient servant,
> (signed) Clarence Arkell
> American Consul

See also code telegram of this date, Nov. 3, 1912.
File 800.

AMERICAN CONSULATE
Ciudad Juarez, Mexico

No. 148   November 20, 1912

SUBJECT: Referring to Americans who recent y claim to have
              been captured and held for ransom by rebels, in
              northern Chihuahua.

The Honorable
     The Secretary of State,
          Washington.

Sir:

I have the honor to refer to recent telegrams and reports sent to the Department concerning Americans who were reported to have been taken and held by the rebels until certain sums of money were paid for their release. The Mexican authorities are complaining bitterly of the imposition (as it is termed by them) which is being perpetrated on both governments by American citizens who make claim of being held for a ransom, and it is charged that Americans go into rebel territory on their own volition for the purpose of treating with said rebels, for the gathering and delivery of cattle for exportation to the United States, and that the monies paid is not for their liberation, but for services rendered. And that the rebels receive much financial aid and encouragement from this source.

It is charged that the rebels gather and turn over to Americans many cattle to which they have no title, and further that Americans furnish ammunition in exchange for cattle.

The Consul after a hasty investigation has failed to discover evidence of ammunition being furnished by the Americans referred to, but of the other allegations there is much evidence of their being well founded. And it is generally admitted in El Paso that the reported holding for a ransom recently of two Americans in which the Department and the public took considerable interest was a deception, and it is no secret that American cattle importers treat with the rebels, and pay them large sums of money.

Aside from the complaints of the nature mentioned there is a decided improvement in the situation in the district, the semi-lawless element are not disturbing the resident Americans, and no great fear is entertained by those people. There is no change in the military situation. It is promised by federal officers here that as soon as the government will furnish mounts, a force sufficient will be put in the field to clear the country of rebels.

I have the honor to be, Sir,

> Your obedient servant,
> (signed) Thos. D. Edwards
> American Consul

AMERICAN CONSULATE
Ciudad Juarez, Mexico

No. 151   December 21, 1912

SUBJECT: Revolutionary Conditions in Mexico.
                Renewed instructions of March 11th.
                11 A.M.

The Honorable
    The Secretary of State,
        Washington.

Sir:

I have the honor of referring to instructions DABSY and DALGY, March 11th, 1912, to report as follows:

1.   This entire district is infected with revolutionary sentiments, and anti-American sentiment, although suppressed to some extent, is popular with ninety per cent of the Mexicans. The majority of the natives are anti-Madero, but becoming tired of war, the majority at present, are in favor of peace.

2.   There are approximately at this time, one thousand American citizens residing in the district, five hundred more doing business or owning interest, but not permanently residing in Mexico. They are generally collected in groups, colonies and mining camps.

3.   They are not armed partially, or at least their supply is very incomplete, no organization worthy of mention, and their experience in the past is not such as to give encouragement to organized armed bodies among themselves.

4.   In case of mob rule of any magnitude, Americans could not resist with much hope of success, and as the last resort, would it be advisable?

5.   There are regularly stationed in this district approximately 3000 federal soldiers under the command of Generals Trucy Aubert and Jose Luz Blanco. They are distributed as follows: at Juarez and the border front 1000. Ojanago 300, Cases Grandes Pearson and Madera about 1000, at small stations along railroads and moving 700. The rebels under Salazar, Rojas, Marcelo Carevo and other less noted leaders have less than one thousand men, they are scattered in bands numbering from 25 to 200 with no regular location. Orozco in my opinion has left the Republic, and also all his leaders who were possessed of any ability or standing as leaders have withdrawn.

6.   It is my opinion that under the present condition in northern Mexico, viz: the rebel forces fast diminishing, and with no means of carrying on their warfare, winning no victories, the loss of moral support, it being the natural disposition of a Mexican to desert a losing man or cause, that there is no reason excepting general slothfulness on the part of the army officers, why the insurrectionists are not completely annihilated, and protection complete. But to keep up a semblance of war, under the army system of Mexico, is to make the position of army officers lucrative as well laudable and infatuating.

I am however, loathe to entertain the possible change in the policy of our government. I am confident that to attempt intervention friendly, or intervention partially, friendly or otherwise would be a failure in so far as restoring peace is concerned, or in protecting life and property. In fact it is my opinion that the slightest evidence of armed intervention would be a signal for the destruction of all American interest that is destructable, before American protection could be brought to bear, and as to the safety of American lives under such circumstances, any conjecture would be unwise. Therefore armed intervention in my opinion means a complete subjection of Mexico as a whole, the taking hold of and controlling the entire governmental affairs, to police every portion of the republic, to keep her people in subjection or a generation, during which time the hatred for us of the whole race will continually be growing (if possible) more venomous.

7.   It is quite impossible to estimate the value of American property or investments which could be destroyed by troops of either side, for the reason principally that the citizenship of the owners of holders of property is difficult to obtain.

I have the honor to be, Sir,

Your obedient servant,
(signed) Thos. D. Edwards
American Consul

T E L E G R A M   R E C E I V E D

> FROM: Mexico City
>
> DATED: January 13, 1913
>
> REC'D: 11:56 p.m.

Secretary of State,
    Washington, D. C.

January 13, 6 p.m.

Calero, recently Mexican Ambassador in Washington, gave a significant interview to EL PAIS, an opposition newspaper, today. He says in part:

> "I resigned as Ambassador because I was not in harmony with the policy of the Government. It is my sincere wish that this policy which I consider mistaken may save the country in the grave crisis through which it is passing. However, my opinion being to the contrary, and since I feel that the Republic is approaching an abyss of misery and desolation, I considered my position as Ambassador unsustainable. Our relations, always delicate with the United States, at this time assume an aspect of extreme delicacy and in my opinion this situation has been brought about by the errors of the present Government."

Interrogated as to the possibilities of intervention, Mr. Calero said:

> "I have strong proofs that the thinking men in American politics oppose all thought of intervention. I know moreover that our neighbors of the north are a great people loving liberty and devoted to the profound sentiments of justice. To speak of intervention as a policy or a tendency of the American people is to speak in error but an unfortunate accident to which we are daily exposed by interior conditions might spontaneously provoke a disaster just as the blowing up of MAINE cost Spain all of her colonial empire."

He speaks of the economic ruin with which the country is threatened as being no longer a possibility but a fulfillment. He evidently attributes all of the errors of the present Government to Pino Suarez-Madero combination and influences.

WILSON

THE TAMPICO TIMES,
May 3, 1913.

"THE FOREIGNER IN MEXICO"
Tampico, Mexico
Saturday, May 3, 1913

"AMERICANS OWN 75 PERCENT OF MEXICO"
****

"Some persons have said that the United States has no good reason to intervene in Mexico unless open war is made upon American citizens; maybe not, but we certainly must protect our property rights," said United States senator A. B. Fall. I had known in a general way that Americans owned a large percentage of the wealth of Mexico, but just to find out what the approximate percentage was, I asked the State Department the other day to furnish me with figures. I was informed that 75 percent of the wealth of Mexico is in the hands of Americans. Mind you, the Americans have a greater property interest in Mexico than the Mexicans themselves. Other foreigners, of course, are credited the remaining 25 percent. So it would appear that Americans should be more vitally concerned about what happens in Mexico than any other people. I do not believe that peace will be maintained there. I do not think continued peace is possible.

The accepted maxim that every nation has the government which it deserves would seem very severe if applied to Mexico under the present regime.

This unhappy country is the prey of ambitious and conscientiousless politicians who are exploiting it for their own selfish purposes. Felix Diaz, an opera coupe hero, whose military achievements have furnished a delightful subject for the comic papers, has been moving heaven and earth to call the elections so that he might become president, in spite of the fact that almost the whole country is in open rebellion. In disappointment has sent in his resignation, but with a string to it. Huerta, whose ambition is to become the dictator of Mexico, has declared against elections under existing conditions, and the fight goes merrily on.

It is a case of the ins and outs. Felix wants to be president with total disregard for the public good, and Huerta wants to hold on as long as he can for the same unworthy motive. In the meantime the country is in a blaze of rebellion and brigandage while the grafting politician follows his profession in search of power and profit.

Since the murder of the lawful elected Madero, conditions have been gradually growing worse and an intimidated press has looked silently on.

But the growing troubles of the Huerta administration have emboldened a few of the Mexico City papers to speak the truth. La Nacion, among others, says:

Lic. Olaguibel has confessed in the chamber that, when they were attacking Don Francisco I. Madero, political maneuvers forbade them to proclaim the merits and extol the virtues of the unfortunate ex-president. These words, which are equivalent to a posthumous tribute, give us an insight into the shamelessness of our professional politicians, who, caring for nothing but the attainment of their ends, turn a deaf ear to the dictates of justice and stifle the voice of conscience, in order to make a living out of their trade, while at the same time paying off their personal grudges or gratifying their wretched amour propre.

"Another of the famous trio, Lozano, called Don Francisco I. Madero an apostle, indulged in a panegyric of the murdered ex-president, and apostrophizing patriotism, he applied to it a name which ordinarily stirs men and lifts them up, but which has been contaminated by so often ensuing from the mouths of politicians.

"And after all these disasters we have made no progress and we see no prospect of a remedy against future catastrophes: for until power [...portions illegible], will continue wholesome in thought, word and deed, until sound political ideas are completely lost and the salvation of the nation becomes impossible.

"We were saying that the insincerity of these politicians had been acknowledged by them either from remorse or in utter shamelessness, and we now have to add that it cannot have been remorse, for when remorse obliges people to confess a sin, it is sincere and moves them to repentance and amendment; so that the confession is made from shamelessness, for in condemning their past stand, they seek to justify their present servility.

"Such is the work of the professional politicians; they have given themselves away, while quarreling among themselves, employing either the transparent euphemism or the brutal jest, but showing, in any case, that they are influenced by private and personal interests, opposed to the interests of our country."

Their ambitions to distract attention from their own little game, in name and forum, are endeavoring to direct public opinion against the foreigner.

What about the foreigner? His money has built the railroads, these great civilizers, which traverse the breadth and length of the land, opened their mines, developed their agricultural and industrial resources, and wherever that money is invested you can see prosperity and well paid and contented labor.

American capital alone in Mexico is represented by over eight hundred millions and other foreign capital in proportion.

Compare the status of the laborer in say Chihuahua and Tampico where vast foreign capital is invested with the parts of Mexico under exclusively Mexican conditions.

In Chihuahua the foreigner has raised wages from twenty-five cents to a dollar and a quarter per day, and in Tampico which is more Americanized than elsewhere in the Republic the lowest wage is a dollar and a quarter a day and from that to five and ten dollars a day for skilled labor, while in Southern Mexico twenty-five cents a day and scrfdom is the rule.

What is the result of this enlightened and benevolent treatment of labor? A happy and contented workman, living with his family in a good home, his children well dressed and educated. Look at the throngs of fashionable appareled children of workmen who frequent our parks and promenades on any equality with their rich neighbors, something that was forbidden to the poor under the degrading tyranny of Porfirio Diaz.

A striking instance of the improved condition of labor under foreign employers was witnessed the other day when the stevedores of this port voted seven hundred and fifty dollars out of their surplus funds and sent it to Mexico City as their contribution to the pacification of the country, and on the first of May, Labor Day, an immense throng of these same stevedores preceded by a squad of mounted police and a brass band paraded the public thoroughfares, clean, well dressed and contented.

These men have no use for revolution and revolutionists and want only to be permitted to pursue their avocation unmolested.

****

Translated from: "REPUBLICA," May 18, 1913.

"AS OTHERS SEE US"
****

"Oh wad some power, the giftei gee us,
To see ourselves as ithers see us;
It wad from money a sorrow free us,
And foolish feeling."   (Burns)

On Friday morning there was placed in our hands an article, said to have been printed in the Tampico Times in its issue of the 3rd. In due time we procured a copy, the reading of which gave us a bad quarter of an hour.

During the long time in which we have been writing for the press, we have used our every endeavour to foster a cordial feeling, a friendly relationship, between the members of the different races reading our paper. The more earnest have we been in this endeavour with the foreigners who have settled in and around this Port, or who may be transiently abiding in it. Whatever our personal feelings may have been, we have never allowed our judgement to become warped in speaking or writing of the undoubted influence exercised by the foreigner in some parts of Mexico, and more particularly in this district, on account of the heavy sums disbursed in the adjacent oil fields.

The author of the article in question, has been imprudent enough to write a long tirade in which every branch of the Mexican Government is vilified, its Chief Executive is classed as an unscruplous assassin, one of its most popular Generals is held up to ridicule, and charged with mercenary motives, while its Congress is said to be a nest of thieving, revengeful and unconscientious politicians. Not content with this, the writer endeavours to make it appear, through the means of some astounding assertions, that the Mexican Nation has no ownership interest in his own country. To quote from the article, "Americans own seventy five per cent of Mexico," "Other foreigners of course are credited with the remaining twenty five per cent." Now seventy five and twenty five are one hundred. Where does the Mexican citizen come in?

The writer goes on to point out, that any and every progress made in this country, has been due to the influence of American gold; that in those sections where American gold is invested, peace and prosperity abound, while in those unhappy sections where the almighty "dollar" has not found its way, poverty and serfdom exist. In a single blow he destroys every spark of self respect and love of country which we Mexicans have in common with other nations.

Considering the matter calmly, we think that perhaps the writer did not understand the enormity of the charges he preferred against the actual administration of the Mexican Republic. Neither did he realize, given the tension existing between the two neighbouring governments, on account of the long deferred American recognition of the Huerta Government, the extremely bitter feeling his article would arouse. There is no feeling so bitter as that produced from a wounded pride, and for a much less violent article than that under consideration, the mob set fire to the Nueva Era building and wrecked all its costly machinery.

While we confess to a feeling of intense indignation engendered by reading the article in question, yet after thinking it over, we are inclined to the belief that there was no real intention of stirring up strife in Tampico, but it was the writer's crude way of expressing his distorted conception of the real status of Mexican affairs. Much of the subject matter was composed of clippings from Mexican papers worked in to appear his own but this after all only makes the wrong done greater, for it reveals a desire to mislead the judgement of its American readers, by reprinting the far fetched phrases of some disgruntled Mexican politician.

****

AMERICAN CONSULATE

Ensenada, L. C., Mexico

No. 240   July 3, 1913

SUBJECT: Political Situation.

The Honorable

  The Secretary of State,

    Washington.

Sir:

I have the honor to report that conditions remain very quiet in this district, with no probablility of any change in the near future. I believe the majority of the people living in this section are in sympathy with the revolutionists of Sonora and the northern part of the Republic, but, there being no agitators here, they are content to let matters take their course without any active steps on their part.

The military force in this district has not changed since my previous report.

A few weeks ago an attempt was made by a few army officers and government employees (all from the central and southern part of Mexico) to form a club in Ensenada to known as the "Club Anti-Gringo". Their intention was to rent a building on the main street and to have a large sign bearing these words placed across its front.

However, learning of this puerile attempt to insult the Americans residing here the Jefe Politico refused to allow the club to be formed, and the matter has now been dropped.

I have the honor to be, Sir,

Your obedient servant,

(signed) Claude E. Guyant

Consul at Salina Cruz,
Acting as Vice Consul at Ensenada.

File No. 800.

T E L E G R A M   R E C E I V E D

FROM: (Chihuahua, Mex.),
          El Paso, Texas

DATED: July 3, 1913

REC'D: July 4, 1913
          9:45 a.m.

Secretary of State,
        Washington, D. C.

American mines at Santa Eulalia have all been forced to close down
because of adverse conditions arising from conflicting control of
Constitutionalists and Federals. It is expected that the smelter of the
American Smelting and Refining Company will close next week for lack
of ore due to isolation from Santa Eulalia. Labor in all the camps is
greatly demoralized because of revolutionary conditions and companies
that continue are operating under greater difficulties than ever known.
The Canadian enterprise of Santa Rosalia known as the Mexican
Northern Light and Power Company will practically suspend June
thirtieth. There appears to be no prospect of early resumption of
communications either north or south. Parties arriving recently from
Torreon report about three thousand Federals there but no early
movement north in force seems to be preparing. The question of food
supplies in this place may become serious after two or three weeks
more.

                              LETCHER.
                         American Consul,
                         Chihuahua, Mexico,
                         June 28, overland to
                         El Paso, Texas.

AMERICAN CONSULATE
Saltillo, Mexico

No. 199   July 5th, 1913

SUBJECT: The vice consul requests certain information
                    concerning the Privileges and Immunities of
                    the consulate.

The Honorable
    The Secretary of State,
        Washington.

Sir:

The vice consul has the honor to inform the Department that
during the past few months, owing to the different political occupations
of the city, and the threatened attacks on the city, the consulate has
been called on a number of times for refuge.

In the way of general instruction the following has been noted:
"Internationa Law Digest: Vol. II page 824, section 301, "It is to be
borne in mind that the consulate does not possess the right of
extraterritoriality, and that while it is an act of humanity to protect
defenseless persons from mob violence and hasty revenge, during the
transition of governments, it is advisable to avoid giving permanent
protection to political refugees, and thus prevent conflicts with the
local authorities." In "Rights and Duties of Consuls" page 48,
paragraph 745, occurs the following: "By various treaties, inviolability
of the consular office and dwelling is expressly secured. This does not
imply that the consular dwelling may be used as asylum."

The vice consul has assumed that Americans, in case of serious
danger, might leave their dwellings and seek the protection of the

consulate, if they so desired, for their persons and their valuables, and that once within the consulate premises, they and their property would be entitled to, and would possess, the same immunity that the government's representative and the government property would possess. Under this presumption, the consulate has at different times, upon request, offered protection and has accepted for temporary safe-keeping, sealed and locked boxes containing valuables. Questions.

1.   Under the paragraph quoted from section 705 "Rights and Duties of Consuls", was the consulate within its prerogatives in such action?

2.   If such protection and refuge may be given Americans, could the same privilege and protection be given, under similar circumstances, to other nationals who are without consular representation?

3.   To what extent could similar privilege and protection be given to Mexicans? Whole families of Mexicans including men, women and children have requested the protection of the consulate.

4.   How far could such privilege and protection be extended to American missionaries and their schools, composed of American teachers and Mexican pupils, or American Sisters of Charity in charge of say, a school of reform for wayward Mexican girls?

5.   What protection or asylum, if any, could be given a Mexican official, who fearing imprisonment by the opposition seeks refuge in the consulate?

6.   What should be the attitude of the consulate in case its protection is asked by a Mexican mother and American wife of a notorious rebel chief, they being in fear of their lives from the government soldiers if rebel forces should enter the city?

I have the honor to be, Sir,

> Your obedient servant,
> (signed) John R. Gilliman
> Vice Consul in charge.

T E L E G R A M   R E C E I V E D

                                        FROM: Verz Cruz, Mexico

                                        DATED: July 7, 1913

                                        REC'D: 10:57 p.m.

Secretary of State,
    Washington, D. C.

    July 7, 5 p.m.
    Wireless from Tampico:
    July 5, 12 midnight. The following telegram has been received from
Consular Agent, Tuxpam, dated July 4, 8 p.m.:

    "A decisive battle was fought yesterday at Cobos, (inserted) three
miles distant and across Tuxpam River from Tuxpam and which is
administration camp of Oil Fields of Mexico Company, American; (end
insert) fighting fierce Cobos. Revolutionists have taken possession of
Furbero railroad which is also company property. Revolutionists have
their head-quarters at Palmasola also company property. Consider it
very dangerous for Americans. My life was threatened."

    Private information indicates NEW HAMPSHIRE arrived Tuxpam this
morning, July fifth. Tampico-Monterey Railroad and telegraph
interrupted today. Revolutionists active in southern Tamaulipas.
Tampico-San Luis Potosi Railroad again resumed. Apparently conditions
are not changed by change of Governors in Vera Cruz and San Luis
Potosi. Embassy advised. MILLER, Consul.

                                        CANADA

T E L E G R A M   R E C E I V E D

                                        FROM: Mexico City

                                        DATED: July 11, 1913

                                        REC'D: 8:42 p.m.

Secretary of State,
    Washington.

    THREE NINETEEN.
    July 11, 1 p.m.

    Department's two seventy-nine, July 10, 6 p.m. When calling to the
attention of the President the Embassy's three thirteen, July 8, 5 p.m.,
and three sixteen, July 9, 5 p.m., his attention should also be called
to the Embassy's three eleven, July 8, 11 a.m., and to the following:
That the transaction of business of any kind by this Embassy with this
Government has now become practically impossible as no attention is
paid to representations concerning protection to either property or life
even when repeatedly made; that Americans have been told by
subordinate officials that they have instructions to discriminate, delay
and ignore all American matters; and that a practical boycott is being
directed by this Government not only against our official
representatives but against individual Americans all over the Republic
who have matters pending with the Government or who require
protection. This is accompanied by a rising tide of bitterness and
resentment which is finding unlicensed expression in the press which is
now exciting the mob and is almost the sole topic of conversation. The
sufferings and losses of Americans in Mexico already received,
incomputable, promise to become infinitely greater and their treatment is
rapidly tending toward persecution. The insolence of public officials to
this Embassy has become intolerable and on Monday I was obliged to say
to the President that unless the Under Secretary of Foreign Affairs was
immediately dismissed for his insolent bearing towards the Embassy, I

should be compelled immediately to take some action that would bring matters to a crisis. This official was dismissed but the general situation remains the same.

The President should understand that in dealing with this situation he is now face to face with grave responsibilities which cannot be evaded by a halting or uncertain policy but only by an action of a firm, formidable and impressive character. One of the two courses indicated in my three sixteen, July 9, 5 p.m., is all I can suggest but perhaps the President may find another more satisfactory remedy for the situation.

HENRY LANE WILSON

T E L E G R A M   R E C E I V E D

FROM: Mexico City

DATED: July 13, 1913

REC'D: July 14, 1913
         9:45 a.m.

Secretary of State,
    Washington.

THREE TWENTY-FIVE.
July 13, 10 a.m.

The anti-American demonstration which was attempted yesterday was prevented by the Government and another one set for today is forbidden. Feeling is running very high and American resentment is very strong. A movement was started yesterday among Americans to request protection from the German Emperor on the ground that our Government neither considered their interests nor afforded them protection. This movement has been arrested for the present. I addressed a note of the severest character to the Foreign Office yesterday relative to the exciting of public opinion and in it I said that I could not permit violence to or abuse of Americans without making use of all the resources in my hands. There were other severe phrases in the note and it had a most salutatory effect as the anti-American demonstration which was to occur yesterday or today was undoubtedly fostered by certain members of the Cabinet. Last night, at the request of the Foreign Office, I gave a very brief memorandum denying the searchlight incident in Guaymas and stating that if any Consul of the United States, referring to Matamoros, had violated established precedents or principles of international law in his attitude toward this Government he would undoubtedly be punished by the Government of the United States. This appears in a mutilated form and as a part of a letter in the press this morning showing that the only method of dealing with these people is with unyielding severity. At the moment of coding this telegram the Embassy has received a telephone message that five hundred people are parading the streets yelling "Death to the Gringoes!" and other opprobrious things.

HENRY LANE WILSON

[T R A N S L A T I O N]

GOVERNMENT OF MEXICO
DEPARTMENT OF FOREIGN AFFAIRS

July 15, 1913

His Excellency
Henry Lane Wilson
    Ambassador Extraordinary and Plenipotentiary of the
       United States of America

Mr. Ambassador:

In note No. 6243-800, dated the 12th instant, Your Excellency states, that you have noted with the greatest concern and some astonishment the remarkable demonstrations of ill will and hostility towards the Government of the United States which have taken place in this metropolis during the last three days. Your Excellency continues to say that the excited and sensational utterances of an irresponsible press reciting occurrences which never occurred and events which never transpired; the supposedly patriotic ebullitions of misguided and tempestuous youth seeking to find expression in denounciation of a friendly power at the risk of the lives of Americans living in this country and who, on the other hand, are in sympathy with their views; and the apathy of those who might guide and restrain public opinion at a time when, for the interest and good name of their own country, they should be active and vigilant, have made a profound impression on that Embassy and have brought it with great reluctance to a realization of the necessity of urging this government to take active and immediate steps looking to the abatement of an entirely unjustifiable public excitement which might easily be made use of by demogogues or the enemies of order, in bringing about conditions in this capital dangerous to all peaceful foreigners.

Your Excellency states that you are obliged to say in the most friendly way that while the Embassy may be under your charge, you cannot permit, without making use of all the resources placed in your hands, indiscriminate and unjustifiable abuse of the American Government, the American people, or Americans resident in Mexico, nor will any act of violence towards Americans, which it is within the power of my Government to prevent, be tolerated or extenuated.

Your Excellency recalls to my mind the circumstance that over half a million Mexicans are living on the other side of the frontier in peace and prosperity and under the protection of the laws of the United States and that these Mexicans are not menaced by public demonstrations nor attacked by the press, injured in their business or threatened with violence.

Your Excellency concludes by saying that with full knowledge of what this Government can and what it cannot do, you must request that the necessary steps guaranteeing to the Americans in Mexico every privilege and as much safety from abuse and violence as the citizens of this Republic enjoy under the laws of the country.

It is a matter of much regret to me, as it is to Your Excellency to refer to the manifestations of bad will on the part of a certain group and of various journals of the capital against the Government of the United States; but I cannot but call Your Excellency's attention to the fact that such manifestations, in so far as the majority of the newspapers and the greater masses of the people are concerned, especially the youth of the schools and the working classes, are not directed against the American nation and much ess against the Americans residing in this capital, which facts perhaps have not reached Your Excellency's knowledge in all the extent of the truth because of the natural excitement of your informants.

Your Excellency states that the Americans who live in Mexico, whose supposed dangers have given rise to the representations I have the honor to reply to, are in perfect sympathy with the mass of the demonstrators and this very thing indicates to what extent their demonstrations will go, as the people know that the American colony of the capital has been able to win the esteem it enjoys and I can without the least doubt assure Your Excellency that if the Americans have enjoyed in Mexico the fullest protection, the same has not been the exclusive result of the vigilance of the Government, but also of the spirit of justice which moves the whole country, even at a time of excitement produced by the acts to which Your Excellency refers and which I am sure would not have caused the excitement of passions, such as we see, if certain representations had been attended to in time when made by the Government of Mexico in the most friendly way and with the desire to present before public opinion in this country the satisfactory results of its diplomatic action near the American Government in order to calm all kinds of animosity.

Your Excellency may be sure, as there are many proofs in support of it, that the Mexican Government spontaneously will at all times prevent the overflowing of popular sentiment against the citizens or representatives of a friendly nation, whatever may be the diplomatic relations with the foreign Government to which they may belong, and Your Excellency may also feel certain that my Government will do nothing that will excite public opinion by giving out events which should remain a secret in the Chancelleries or by presenting others in an adulterated form.

I cannot refrain from mentioning and examining the latest events, in order to make it completely clear as regards the reference made in Your Excellency's note.

The case of the Mexican flag insulted in Tucson was not published by the Mexican Government but on the contrary, the statements of the Department of Foreign Relations very eloquently show the desire to appease public opinion notwithstanding that, as Your Excellency knows it, it has been necessary to resort to all the means of persuasion in order not to show in all its broadness the lack of an active and energetic desire on the part of the United States to satisfy the just demands of the Mexican Government.

With reference to the case of Consul Johnson I shall say only that the events having occurred about the middle of June and the details of the same having been published since then with regard to the attempt to have the military band held at Brownsville pass into the ranks of the rebels, as suggested by the above Consul, it has not been the Mexican Government which has published the matter in the press and it is not to blame if its efforts have been without a satisfactory reply to this day. To withdraw the exequatur of the above Consul, though perfectly justifiable, would have meant to deprive the Government of the United States of the occasion it had to show its spirit of impartiality and its good will towards this country and it would have tended to exasperate the sentiments of the people.

In the case of the conduct of the Commander of the <u>S. S. Pittsburg</u> some representations have been made to the Government of the United States, not precisely with reference to the direction given to the rays of the search lights at the time of the fight between Government and rebel forces, but in regard to certain maneuvering of a suspicious character which might not indicate complicity, but a sign of the sympathy which, according to evidence generally obtained by the Embassy, exists between American residents of Sonora and the rebels operating in that state. On the other hand the acts executed by the Commander of the <u>Pittsburg</u> were so public that no official declaration was needed to have them become the property of the press.

As Your Excellency may see, the whole of this affair is not a matter of fictitious doings to excite public opinion, but of a status of deep excitement the cause of which is well known to Your Excellency, which you implicitly recognize when you say that the impartial and just American colony resident of this city is in close sympathy with the views of the demonstrators to whom you refer.

It is not my intention to defend the press which maliciously tends to create a state of disturbance in the conscience and which it preserves in it by means of false reports and inflamatory statements; but if such would be the theme of this note, there is no doubt but what the Mexican press would be the less guilty, inasmuch as Your Excellency knows the amount and intensity of the insults, slander and offenses of all kinds which the press of the United States has been publishing during the past three years against men and groups of parties of my country and even against the whole nation, encouraged sometimes by the opinion of persons of political influence in the United States, and on no few occasions by correspondents who live among us and who claim to be eye-witnesses of acts of their own invention or fancy, thus contributing to the torrent of misguided opinion of which Your Excellency has been one of the victims.

I will not make a comparison between the privileges and advantages enjoyed by Mexican and American emigrants, as from such comparison Your Excellency's compatriots would not surely be under disadvantage. In this respect Your Excellency's indications shall always be, as in the past, carefully attended to, without taking into consideration the equal treatment received by our nationals in the United States, because even though in many cases they may be treated differently on account of their origin or position, because to do likewise would not be the means of remedying a deplorable condition, but to cause a descent in the level of the obligations which Mexico has to protect all foreigners residing within its territory.

I renew to, etc., etc.

Carlos Pereyra

AMERICAN CONSULATE

Tampico, Tamps

No. 818   July 19, 1913

SUBJECT: Confidential -- Political Conditions.

The Honorable
    The Secretary of State,
        Washington.

Sir:

    I have the honor to enclose herewith a copy of letter which is
apparently being sent out to various members of Congress in the United
States.

    I have the honor to be, Sir,

                              Your obedient servant,

                              (signed) Clarence Arkell

                              American Consul.

Enclosure with Despatch No.818, July 19, 1913.
Copy of "Circular" letter which is being copied and
forwarded direct or indirectly to Members of
Congress.

Dear Sir & Friend:

Knowing your well known policy of at all times being a champion of the people, always being ready and willing to take their part, and believing that you fully understand our reasons in coming to Mexico, and that if for no other reason, we are excusable for so doing as we are "sons of our forefathers", who by their efforts made it possible to increase the stars in our beloved flag, and added much territory to our holdings, and the further fact that we came here to escape the congested conditions of many portions of the United States, and take advantage of the cheap land, unexcelled climate, and great productiveness of the soil, and our urgent need to make for our children a home, we appeal to you to take our part with our Government who up to this date, has given us no protection and who has told us to "get out if we considered that we are in danger" and later after receiving thousands of petitions, and letters, to say nothing of personal appeals, they declare through the press, that they will not alter their policy toward Mexico, no matter what happens.

These statements from our Government have been construed by the majority of citizens of this country, and her waring factions, that we cannot look to our Government for any protection, and they treat us accordingly. Prior to 1910 Mexico had a stable Government, and we had ample protection, and were well treated, and therefore thousands of American citizens came to this country to that advantage of the many inducements offered for investments, etc. Many of these were people of small means, and in many instances sold their all in the United States and came here investing in small tracts of land, and after building for their families a home, began to develop their holdings. They were very successful, and were just beginning to make money and live easy, when the revolution started. Since that time, the bandit - rebels, took their guns and ammunition, then their work stock and provisions, and made life so unbearable that they were forced to abandon their homes and leave the country, some at their own expense, but invariably with their last dollar, and others by the efforts of the Red Cross Society.

In thousands of instances, [many] were too old to begin life over again, and have no means of making a decent living in the States. It was impossible for them to stay for they had nothing with which to work their land, and as murder, theft, robbery, arson and rapine, were so prevalent that they knew they were unsafe, therefore sought "safety in flight" leaving their all here to be further demolished by the rabble, who have been armed by the one side or the other. Some were not so fortunate, as to have the chance to get out, for they are in jail, and others are dead, and unless something is done quickly there will be more. It is not our wish to try to inflame your mind, or influence our Government wrongfully, but we do ask justice, and protection because as free born American citizens, we think that we are entitled to it as such.

No matter the course the U. S. Government may pursue, they cannot escape the final responsibility, of acting in some way in Mexico. The proof of this is that matters have grown steadily worse, until anarchy has increased until it has reached every state and jurisdiction in the whole Republic.

The army and rebel ranks are filled with at least 90% of it is the ignorant people of the country, who have been taught to shoot and handle guns, and the army is paid an average of $1.50 (pesos) per day and the rebels are receiving $2.00 per day and have license to rob, loot and steal at will. The same people have only been used to a wage of from 25 cts. to one peso per day for their work, and these prices were all that they were worth on account of their methods of work and of the general conditions of the markets and of the country, for the product of the soil, therefore it is a sure thing that they will never be willing to return to work until some kind of an "Iron Hand" is placed over them compelling them to lay down their arms and return to the peaceful walks of life. The rebel leaders in order to bring them to their side have offered them many impossible things and they expect if they win a full compliance with the promises made them, and when this cannot be done they are up in arms again, in a long drawn out civil war against their government. Such was the case after the Madero triumph. The Government in order to hold its own has been compelled to in a measure with these promises with others probably not so radical but ruinous to comply with, but have made it plain that if they win they will compel them to return to work and to stop their depredations on the country, therefore even if the Government wins temporarily, it will only be a respite and the warfare will continue. In many sections of the country all work has been stopped, and thousands of men thrown out of employment, and as they depend on their daily labor they have nothing to eat and their families are suffering. Naturally they begin to steal and rob which places them in the rebel bandit ranks or they commit some crime or show their sympathy for the rebels and are forced into the army.

The majority join the rebels because they can make more by their methods than by being under army discipline, and only receiving their per-diem. It is strange to relate, but nevertheless perfectly true that the rebel ranks only represent a very small percentage of the population of Mexico, (in fact net 1% of the population) but the remainder of the people are sitting idly by, seemingly paralized with fear or indifference, and make no effort to right matters. The middle and high class people are not participating on either side and will not do so.

It is a common occurrence for a few bandits to come in to a town or hacienda of several hundred or thousand population, and rob, murder, loot and rape to their hearts content, and the populace if not afraid to so ask the Government for protection. The Rebel bandits are divided up into small squads as a rule, and operate in this manner coming together when they see that they can win against the Federals and as it is impossible for the Government to give protection as they cannot employ the same method of warfare, for the reason that their army is made up of probably 20% criminals or sympathizers to the other side, and if they divide up in squads they lose them to their opponents. The rebels all have horses and the best that the country affords, while much of the Federal army and infantry and compelled to travel on foot or by rail. Infantry on foot cannot keep up with the rebels and one bandit can tear up enough railroad track in two hours with 100 lbs. of explosive and a box of matches that will impede the advancement of a thousand soldiers for a week.

To give you an idea of how they proceed will call your attention to the Matamoros battle. The Government could not keep a very strong force there to protect the town for they were needed worse elsewhere. The rebels destroyed the track and massed a sufficient force to take the town and it was impossible for the Government to reinforce their forces for the reason that the other rebel bands kept them annoyed and harassed at other nearby points and the railroad track being torn up they could not get help there in time.

If they pursue their regular tactics, they will take everything in sight and do their worst, and then evacuate the town when a sufficient force of Federals appear. The same method was employed at Zacatecas and other cities they have taken. The Government is wholly unable to give protection to any one for a certainty, and are on the defensive all over the Republic.

The present Government, nor any other they can establish can win, for to do so they will have to disarm and force the opposition to return to their peaceful walks of life and work and establish a strict execution of the law. The rebels, even if they win, will have to do the same thing, and they cannot do so for if it is right now to pursue their present methods they cannot hope to force their own people to do different under their administration.

I will not attempt here to give you a detailed statement of the thousands of outrages that have been committed on the Mexican people and the foreigners in Mexico, and their property interests but will refer you especially to the reports from the American Consuls from all over Mexico during the last three years, and will ask that you carefully study them and act accordingly. If you will get a list of the people who were taken out of this country by the noble Red Cross Society and write them, I feel sure that your heart will be moved in their behalf and that you will lay diplomacy aside, and use your best efforts to have our Government come to our immediate relief. I say immediate for if it is put off much longer there will be no use to do anything for we will be completely ruined and probably dead.

The lenient policy of the U. S. Government so as considered by the rank and file of the Mexican people is "Cowardice," and they in many instances, personally and through their press, say so publicly and treat us accordingly. We are less respected here than any other nationality by many of the Mexican people.

Many of us have been cooped up for months in the principal cities of Mexico to escape the outrages of the rebels and bandits and have left our properties unprotected and at the mercy of the lawless bands that infest the country.

We have concluded to appeal to our friends in Congress and the Senate and if we do not get relief to take our case direct to the people of the United States, knowing full well that when they realize our deplorable condition, and daily insults and injuries that are being heaped upon us they will take decisive action. Our history teaches us that they have never failed their brothers when in distress, and we have full faith in them now, and believe they will act before they are forced to undergo another "Maine", "Alamo" or "Goliad" massacre.

Thanking you in advance, beg to remain, as ever,

Signed by over one thousand American citizens whose names appear on like petitions now on file in the Department of State at Washington, D. C., from this the Tampico Consular District.

Faithfully yours.

[Unsigned]

REPORT OF M.A. LEACH

Mexican Situation as Strikingly and fearlessly portrayed by

M. A. LEACH,

a prominent business and club man of San Francisco, California, who has been residing in Mexico for the past three years, and is now in Washington, D. C.

States all of his Mexican interests have been ruined and swept away by so-called rebels, therefore not afraid to speak out and tell the world what he knows.

****

Mr. Leach hands us the following news item to publish, stating in so doing that he believes it is the urgent and solemn duty of the press to give the Mexican situation even more publicity than has heretofore been done.

"Until I arrived in San Francisco July 13th, this year, on steamer Sidney, with some eighty-one other Americans from Durango, Mexico, via Mazatlan, I had not seen a United States newspaper since the 11th of March, there not having been any railroad communication with the outside world since that date. Our party having to make a ten day journey over land to Mazatlan to get out of the country. Since my return I have daily read all the leading papers dwelling on the Mexican situation, have talked to many prominent business men and United States Officers, and have wondered at the seeming lack of information displayed by a large part of our people including our State Department, of what is really going on in a large part of Mexico and what is necessary to be done to put an end to the wanton killing of innocent men, women and children, almost unlimited outraging of young girls and women and tremendous destruction of property. Living as I have for the past three years in the states of Chihuahua and Durango, the hot-bed of the trouble, I have been forced to go through many trying experiences and to witness many revolting spectacles. The worst, however, that I have seen was what took place in the city of Durango, after its capture on June 18th, by the forces of Tomas Urbina, Calixtro Contreras, Domingo and Mariano Arrieta and Orestes Perada, numbering in all some 4,200 so-called Maderistis. No sooner had these men entered the city then they began breaking into all the Cantinas (saloons) drinking such liquor as they found there, after which the wholesale sacking and looting of the entire city began. Not a single store escaped being completely sacked. The largest stores "La Suiza" (German), Fabrica de Francia and Francia Maritima (French), and Durango Clothing Company (American), were burned after being sacked, and many others, entailing a property loss of over 10,000,000 pesos. All prisoners from jails and state penitentiary, some 400 in number, were turned loose and all criminal and land records burned. Not content with this all houses were entered and much loot taken and damage done. Scores of Mexican people were shot down and dragged through the streets of the city, which I witnessed in the eight days I remained after the city was captured.

Rogers Palmer, an Englishman, twenty-five years of age, employed by Construction Department, National Railways, was killed because he failed to open a safe to which he did not have the combination. Carlos Von Brandis, a wealthy mining man, and L. W. Elder, owner of a large Hacienda, both Americans, were seriously wounded by a bomb used to force the door of the McDonald Institute, where many of the foreigners had assembled by pre-arrangement for their mutual protection, all inside, some 150 in number, then being lined up against the wall and threatened with execution unless a certain sum of money was immediately raised and all horses, arms and ammunition were delivered, which the foreigners were forced to do to save their lives. H. W. Stepp, a civil engineer, American, was shot through one leg because he failed to pay over the sum of 500 pesos which he did not have. A. W. Laurilaut, an English subject, owner of a large Hacienda was taken out of his home, located two blocks from Urbina's headquarters on the Plaza and after being conducted to the outskirts of the city, through the main streets, was stripped of all his clothing, badly beaten, shot in the side, and left for dead. These are but a few instances of what I personally saw and know about that took place in that illfated city by the forces heretofore mentioned, acting without restraint. Words can never picture the scenes that were daily enacted before our eyes and I have not attempted to do more than mention some of the incidents that happened in Durango, which is one of the oldest and richest cities in the Republic of Mexico, having a population of between 40 and 50,000 people; it having been defended by about 800 Federals, 600 state troops, and 600 volunteers. The latter composed of the best people of the city, who had everything to fight for that a man could have. The lives and honor of their families. Their own lives and property. Yet in the twelve hours of firing, you cannot call it fighting, preceding the capture of the city, less than forty were killed and wounded on both sides, with over six thousand men engaged, which will give you a fair idea of how they fight in Mexico. Most of the soldiers and volunteers escaped. Many of the latter leaving their families to the mercy of the fiends who entered the city; although a large number of the women sought safety in the Archbishop's palace, which was respected up to the time I left, although the Bishop had been taken prisoner and held for a ransom of 500,000 pesos. All three banks were looted, namely Banco Nacional, Banco Londres and Mexico and Banco Durango. Hundreds of women and girls were taken from their homes and outraged, it being heartrending to hear their screams of anguish and when I tell you this was all premeditated it seems almost unbelievable, yet such was the case, as you will see. When the looting first started, I went with the American Consul, Theo. C. Hamm, W. C. Bishop, former owner of the Telephone Company, to see the General known to be in charge, Tomas Urbina, to arrange, if possible, for a guard for the different Consulates and places of refuge of the foreigners. I also wanted a guard for my two stores, the Durango Mercantile Company and American Grocery Company. We succeeded in reaching Urbina, after being robbed in the streets of what money we had in our clothes. Urbina advised us that he could do nothing until 24 hours had elapsed, as his men had been given that length of time to do as they desired in the city, in payment of their services, and nothing was done to stop the men either during the first twenty-four hours or afterwards, with the exception that on the third day a guard was obtained from the Arrietas for the Consulates.

Mr. Graham, English Consul, several days after the city was taken, called upon Urbina, and requested that the men who had killed Palmer be punished. He was told that no investigation was necessary as the killing of Palmer took place in the twenty-four hours allotted to the men, and therefore nothing would be done.

What happened in Durango is but a repetition of what happened when Sombrete, Zacatecas, Parrall and other cities were taken, by these so-called Constitutionalists, and will continue to happen as long as these brutes are left living. These are some and a fair sample of the people that our Government is talking about meditating with. Outside of the State of Sonora there is no revolution in Mexico. Our people have but to go there and travel through the country to substantiate this statement. There are, however, innumerable bandit bands, such as Urbina, in Durango, Pancho Villa, in Chihuahua, the latter being one of the biggest cut-throats in all Mexico; a man, who has to my personal knowledge, raped scores of young girls, looted Parrall and robbed, killed and destroyed wherever he had an opportunity. I personally have been twice robbed by this man and his band. This is the great and brave man, pictured in some of our papers as the leader and head of all Constitutionalists in the State of Chihuahua, a man who Madero had to keep bribed month by month to stand by him. As far as Carranza in Coahuila is concerned, his men behave no better than the others. So we must judge him by their acts. In the south, Zapata is too well known to need any comment.

These men are not fighting for a principle, as some people would lead us to believe. They care nothing for Madero or any other man. What they are after is something for nothing. The ignorant poor against the rich, seeking to obtain by force of arms what they are unable to obtain through their ignorance and dislike for work. They have been urged and I have heard their leaders address them many times to take by force of arms property wherever found; that the mines, Haciendas, timber, and other property owned by foreigners and Mexicans should rightfully be theirs, and ignorant as the majority of the masses are they believe this to be right and will not discontinue, no matter who is President of Mexico, until they are forced to do so, which owing to so many now being under arms will be an impossible task for any Government in Mexico to accomplish without outside help. And God help the people remaining in Mexico if our Government removes the restriction prohibiting the free importation of arms and ammunition by all parties. If we do this we can well call ourselves murderers in the first degree. No man unless he lives in Mexico a number of years can understand the Mexican race or the situation as it really exists. You must rub elbows for a long time with the Peons who make up at least 80 per cent of the Mexican people before you can understand them. I know them because I have dealt with and employed many thousands of them in the past three years. I have personally met many times all the principle leaders in the field in the north, outside of Sonora, and know what kind of men they are and what motives are prompting them to continue fighting and when I say to you that Mexico will never be pacified except with outside help in men and cash by some such plan as advocated by Henry Lane Wilson who knows the Mexican people and conditions there and has the support of 90 percent of the foreigners in that country; I am telling you what every foreigner in Mexico would tell you if he dared to do so.

If Huerta and his Government were objectionable to us, why did he not say so in the beginning, and then and there insist on a change, or step in and settle things ourselves. Huerta would probably have been wiser to let some other man take the provisional Presidency, but he felt, and rightly too, that none but a strong man could handle the situation and had more confidence in himself than in any other, which is but natural. As President Diaz said when leaving Mexico, "They will find that I ruled Mexico in the only way the people are yet capable of being ruled." Time and events have certainly borne out the truth of this statement. Mexico will not be ready for anything else for a half century to come.

I know many Mexican people, and outside of those holding some salaried position with the Government, they who own properties and have something at stake, from the man who owns but a few acres of ground and head of cattle, to the man who owns thousands, want outside armed assistance realizing as they do that the irresponsible and uneducated masses are arrayed against them, and being so largely in the majority if given arms and allowed to continue will make a perfect Hell of all Mexico, and ruin all, having their all invested there.

President Diaz invited foreign investments, realizing that it was necessary for the development of the country. Madero and all his so-called followers, from the beginning, have told the foreigners that they were not wanted, that Mexico was for Mexicans. I heard him make that speech in Madero, Mexico. We have been told by our Government several times to leave Mexico if we felt we were in danger, but when a man has a family to support, his home and business in Mexico, can you expect him to leave everything behind him and go out into the world and begin all over again?

Our Government has parleyed long enough. It is time for action. The Huerta Government has the support of the bulk of the better people of Mexico and should be recognized and assisted with all the forces at our command to speedily end this reign of anarchy, it cannot be called anything else; or we should intervene and set up a Protectorate over all Mexico, as we have successfully done elsewhere. Our Government is losing the esteem and respect of the civilized world by its weak-kneed policy in Mexico. If our worthy President but knew how we were being ridiculed and laughed at by this lack of action on the part of our Government, how we are going to be placed in an embarrassing situation with foreign powers, through the Americans of Mexico getting up a petition to the English government to take a hand in speedily doing something that will relieve the situation, which I happen to know is the case, and which measure they feel that they must adopt although repulsive, through lack of support from their own Government. If President Wilson could have seen our flags and that of other nations shot at, totally disregarded and trailed in the dust, as I have seen, and know how we are scorned and looked down on in Mexico today as a lot of cowards, for putting up with the insults heaped upon us he would, I feel certain, show that he is a man of the hour to uphold the honor of the American nation and its people by applying the inevitable remedy. If our President will not do this, it is time for Congress to do its duty and order the work done, laying aside for the moment all else before it, and thereby save the lives of many hundreds more of people and millions of dollars of property which is almost daily being wasted. Hundreds of people can be quickly found to substantiate what I have written and I know I am voicing the views and feelings of all foreigners in Mexico, in this letter.

[Undated typewritten report, 1913.]

- end -

I N D E X

220

Oaxaca
  outbreaks continue in, 66;
  protection of foreigners
    in, 95

Occidental Construction Company
  letter from President of, 13-16

Oil Fields of Mexico Company
  private train of taken, 169;
  battle fought at, 190

Ojeda, General
  involved in skirmishes with
    rebels, 110

Olivera, General
  believed to be behind guerrilla
    movement, 105

Oluta
  difficulties in obtaining
    laborers from, 131-132

Omealca
  bandits committing depredations
    in, 126

Orizaba
  frequent changes of officials
    in, 17;
  unsatisfactory conditions in
    mills & factories of, 121

Orozco, General Pascual
  sentiment toward, 29;
  forces of may become dis-
    couraged, 76;
  troops of bitterly anti-
    American, 82;
  is receiving financial aid of
    wealthiest men in Mexico, 86;
  considers himself leader of
    "Liberal movement", 104

Oxner, Albert
  reports general satisfaction
    throughout Mexico, 101

Ozuluama
  government in control of, 168

Pacific Ocean, 16

Palmasola
  revolutionists' headquarters
    at, 190

Palmer, Rogers
  killing of, 207

Palos Blancos
  Americans discourage robbers
    at, 47

Panama, 14, 71

Panuco
  is to be abandoned, 110

Parkinson, F.B. (assistant
manager of Utah Mexican Rubber
Company)
  is prepared to leave Mexico,
    108

Paso de Chicoacan
  bandits move to, 87-88

Paso del Macho
  bandits committing depreda-
    tions in, 126

Pavon Gallegos, Antonio
  malicious character of, 132;
  can be captured at Santa Rosa,
    133;
  is instigator of much trouble,
    134

Perada, Orestes
  forces of in Durango, 206-207

Pereyra, Carlos
  letter of concerning Mexican
    feelings toward U.S. and
    U.S. citizens, 193-199

Persians in Mexico
  many seek U.S. citizenship, 97

Pinto Suarez, Jose
  displaces Vasquez Gomez as
    Vice President, 64

Plan de las Hayas
  taken by rebels, 148

224

Playa Vicente
  rebels camped near, 138, 142;
  raid upon in preparatory stages,
    140

Poloney, Colonel Juan A.
  forces under command of, 107

Puebla
  outbreaks continue in, 66;
  division of authority in, 76;
  situation worse in, 82;
  rebels in will move against
    Mexico City, 84

Queretaro
  relative calm in, 76

Quixote, Don, 15

Ramirez, Alba de
  connected with disturbances in
    Tampico, 74

Redo Company
  employees of return to U.S., 46

Republica
  attacks article on American
    investment in Mexico, 183-184

Rio Verde
  bandits surround, 92

Rojas, Antonio
  robbing in Chihuahua, 29

Roman Catholic Church in Mexico,
56

Roosevelt, Theodore (President of
United States)
  stated that people in U.S. knew
    little of Mexico, 100

Root, Elihu, 100

Salina Cruz
  vessel should be sent to, 33

San Antonio
  Vasquez Gomez is in, 28;
  intervention anticipated in, 156

San Dieguito
  American colony of threatened,
    91

San Gabriel
  rebels reported near, 138

San Juan
  forces sent from, 87;
  batallion revolts in, 87;
  forces stationed at, 107;
  yellow fever in, 109

San Lorenzo
  bandits committing depreda-
    tions in, 126

San Luis Potosi
  relative calm in, 76;
  rebel operations increase in
    & Americans leave, 91-94;
  mistreatment of Americans in,
    96-98

Santa Cecilia
  reports of rebels in, 138

Santa Eulalia
  American mines close at, 187

Santa Rosa
  Pavon can be captured at, 133,
    134

Sayago, Domingo, 148

Shafter, J.N.
  letter of concerning possible
    U.S. intervention, 156-158

Shanklin, Arnold (U.S. Consul
General, Mexico City)
  letter to reporting conditions
    in Oaxaca, 95, 105-106;
  letter to concerning state of
    Mexico, 153-155

Shepardam, Orliff
  robbed by rebels, 45-46

Sierra Juarez
  campaign against rebels in not
    begun, 117

225

Sinaloa
anarchy exists in, 22;
crisis in, 31-32;
is endangered, 76;
situation worse in, 82;
Calero reports "some unrest"
in, 103

Sinaloa Land Company
Americans employed by suffer
assaults, 44

Sochiapa
reports of rebels in, 138

Sonora
anarchy exists in, 22;
is not involved with arrangement among border states, 66;
may be taken by militants, 75

Spain, 15
influence of in Mexico, 57

Spanish in Mexico, 156
are prepared to defend themselves, 78;
many leave Mexico, 97

Spanish-American War, 15

Stafford, C.J.
robbed by rebels, 44

Tabasco
quiet in, 76;
order being kept in, 107-109

Taft, William H. (United States
President)
letter to concerning Mexican
sentiment toward Americans,
13-16;
proclamation of concerning
disturbances in Mexico, 49-
50, 97, 99;
proclamation of unnecessary, 55;
letter to expressing gratitude
for non-intervention by U.S.,
159-162

Tamaulipas
invaded by insurgants, 36;
dangerous outbreaks in, 76;
plans for taking of, 168-169

Tamaulipas Bank
delivers money to War Commission in Tuxpam, 169

Tamazula
real estate in owned by
Occidental Construction Co.,
13

Tampico, Ciudad
political conditions in, 73-
74;
revolutionists moving toward,
167-169;
wages paid in, 181

Tampico-San Luis Potosi Railroad
operations of resume, 190

Tampico Times, 73

Texas, 71

Tierra Blanca
conditions in & around, 149-
150, 152;
rurales sent from, 151;
soldiers sent to, 152

Tlaxcala
outbreaks continue in, 66;
division of authority in, 76

Tompkins, _____
attacked & robbed by Mexicans,
41

Topolobampo Bay
gunboat needed in, 32

Torreon
anti-American sentiment in,
22;
rebels order surrender of, 28-
29;